CONFESSIONS OF AN OUTSOURCER

TIMOTHY BRANTINGHAM

CONFESSIONS OF AN OUTSOURCER

AN INSIDER EXAMINES THE OPENINGS, CLOSINGS, FORTUNES, AND FALLOUT OF THE CHINA TRADE

Published by Advantage Books, Charleston, South Carolina.
An imprint of Advantage Media.

Printed in the United States of America.

10 9 8 7 6 5 4 3 2 1

ISBN: 979-8-89188-310-9 (Paperback)
ISBN: 979-8-89188-311-6 (eBook)

Library of Congress Control Number: 2026903414.

Cover design by Matthew Morse.
Layout design by Ruthie Wood.

03-03-2026 12:1

Dedicated to the memory of my great-grandmother, Isabella French DeVol, who first went to China in 1896, and her husband, George, who joined her in 1900.

To my siblings, Jeanne, David, and Jonathan, who paved the first roads into a reopened China in the 1980s, costing themselves no small amount of blood, sweat, and tears.

And to my business partner, Matt Carroll, who helped this liberal artist find a meaningful vocation in business.

CONTENTS

BRING JOBS HOME
NO MORE CHINA TRADE

ACKNOWLEDGMENTS

A hearty thank-you to Advantage Media Group for taking me on and showing me the ropes of book publishing. Thanks to Harper Tucker for the encouragement and guiding wisdom, to Elizabeth Kennedy for her editorial skills (and patience), and to Matthew Morse for the cover design. Thanks to Allison Vittardi and the team for the guidance on building a great platform—a home—for other global nomads like me.

To Mark Leichliter, a very deep thank-you for settling me down and helping me conceive, frame, and wordsmith this book. I couldn't have done it without you.

Thanks to Dr. Eric Thun, associate professor of Chinese Business Studies at Said Business School, University of Oxford.

To my family members who truth-checked me, thank you. Especially Jeanne and Peter Hayes and Lee Brantingham.

And finally, thanks to my wife, Mariko, who never second-guesses my search for meaning and the inevitable twists and turns it brings into our lives.

Like this one …

BRING JOBS HOME
NO MORE CHINA TRADE

ABOUT THE AUTHOR

Timothy Brantingham brings three decades of experience in supply chain management and US–China trade to his writing on global commerce. Born in Taiwan to three generations of Ohioan Asia-based missionaries, his personal and professional lives have been centered around bridging cultures.

He holds a BA in East Asian studies from William & Mary, an MA in Buddhist studies from the University of Hong Kong, and an MBA from the University of Oxford. Fluent in Mandarin, he has lived and worked his entire career in mainland China, Hong Kong, and Japan, advising companies large and small on scaling operations in Asia, particularly in renewable energy and industrial manufacturing.

Now based in Honolulu with his family, Timothy writes and speaks on US–Asia trade relations and the human stakes of globalization. You can follow his work at *The Global In-Betweenist* (www.globalinbetweenist.com).

BRING JOBS HOME
NO MORE CHINA TRADE

AUTHOR'S NOTE

In this book, you will read about many companies and individuals in both the US and China, some associated with my own work and some not, whose stories help illustrate vital aspects of US trade with China. As this topic is politically and economically sensitive for all involved—in both the US and China—all names have been changed, and sometimes industries have been altered as well.

Those who are Chinese nationals are referenced by their formal surnames, as is the custom in Chinese society.

Please note the manuscript for this book was finalized in late 2025. In international trade, and trade with China in particular, things change very fast. By the time you read this book, some situations and realities may have changed, either slightly or radically, which may make some points less relevant than they were when I wrote this book.

I will continue the conversation on this content on my online platform: The Global In-Betweenist (www.globalinbetweenist.com).

Join me there to see these arguments updated and for further case studies, commentary, and related content.

BRING
JOBS
HOME
NO
MORE
CHINA
TRADE

INTRODUCTION

FROM CHINA HAND TO CHINA HEEL

I am a birthright American citizen. I am also a lifelong China guy. I'm not a China watcher, theoretician, or academic pontificating about China from twenty thousand feet in the air. My China experience comes with thirty years of factory grease under my fingernails, thirty years of *baijiu,* a sorghum liquor, jet-fueling through my liver, and thirty years of wrestling with national prejudices, in both the US and China.

I have lived a decade in mainland China itself and two decades in Hong Kong, and I was born and raised in Taiwan. At the age of eighteen, I lived in the US for the first time in my life while attending William & Mary. I have lived more of my life within the realms of Greater China than I have in the US. And while this statement may garner deep suspicion from my American readers, I must simply declare here: I am deeply connected to both sides, and I love them both.

That is why I am writing this book.

My Chinese friends sometimes slap me on the back and call me a China hand (中国通 Zhōngguó tōng). The term originally referred to nineteenth-century foreign merchants who lived and worked in China's treaty ports. Over time, it came to describe any foreigner with deep knowledge of China's language, culture, and people. I don't know if I've earned the distinction of being a China hand—it's not a title you can give yourself—but after three decades working on the ground in China, I'm at least China-handed.

China-"handedness" is also kind of in my DNA. I come from a line of Quaker missionaries who made understanding China central to their careers. My great-grandparents set up a medical practice and a Friends meetinghouse on the outskirts of Nanjing in 1900. My grandmother was born there. She did a stint at Shanghai American School in 1910–1911, boarding with Pearl S. Buck, before returning to the US after her father died of cholera.

That grandmother had every intention of going to China as a missionary, but the 1930s were a dangerous time in China, so she and her young family went to India instead. That's where my mother grew up, spending her holidays on the plains of Madhya Pradesh and her school terms at Woodstock School in the foothills of the Himalayas.

By the time my parents were ready to take up their missionary service, the church community established by my great-grandparents, which had previously been centered in Nanjing, fled with Chiang Kai-shek's Nationalist forces to Taiwan to escape the impending Communist victory. And so that is where my parents went to serve: Taiwan. That's where I was born and where I grew up.

The Taiwan I grew up in was American supported, both militarily and economically. It was the time of two Chinas: a so-called Free China based in Taiwan under Chiang Kai-shek and a Red China on the mainland under Mao. Any foreign magazine that came to our house, such as *TIME* or *Newsweek*, if it were to contain mention of Red China in its pages, would be blacked out by the censors. I grew up loving the so-called Free China government in Taiwan and distrusting the Red Menace on the mainland, though I knew almost nothing about it.

Nixon's 1972 trip to China, the first by a sitting US president, led to formal US recognition of the People's Republic of China in 1978. Within eight years, my siblings were among the first business folk to set up trading and manufacturing enterprises in China.

I was in college in the US during the late 1980s and early 1990s, a time of budding enthusiasm for all things China. Chinese studies majors sprouted up in numerous universities, and there was a sense that a new moment in history had arrived: China, that great prize of geopolitics, was finally opening to American interests.

I graduated college fully fluent in Mandarin and with a degree in East Asian studies. My supervising professor, Jian Xiaoping, who went from being a Guangzhou taxi driver to an Ohio State PhD, told me on the eve of my leaving for Shanghai, "Wow—what you will see and experience in China, Tim, will be unprecedented. This is new history."

He was right. What I saw was unprecedented. I witnessed an industrial behemoth emerge from practically nothing to form cities filled with skyscrapers as millions of people moved out of the rice paddies. And all that was just within the span of my twenties and thirties. After a brief break to study Buddhism at the University of Hong Kong, in my late thirties, I started a supply chain management and manufacturing business with an old high school friend from Taipei American School. We rode the wave to peak China—that time in the mid-2010s when the US–China trade relationship was cruising on all cylinders. Everyone needed the China price—they needed the sheer scale of what Chinese factories could produce, and they needed the iterative speed that developing new products in China could bring to a company's competitive stance. Our pipeline of new business was always robust.

By my forties, China was already a global competitor to the US.

As I write this book in 2025, China is the second-largest economy in the world. And that outsourcing we hear so much about (and which I had a part in pushing along) is something so common that we take it for granted. You likely need look no further than the label on your shirt or the serial number on your electronic device for a reminder. Trade in goods between the US and China increased from less than $100 billion in 1999 (prior to China joining the World Trade Organization in 2001) to a peak of $690 billion in 2022. China surpassed Germany to become the world's largest exporter in 2009.[1] Now, China exports four times what Germany does.

When in history has this kind of growth ever happened in the span of one man's career?

Now that I am in my mid-fifties, the early enthusiasm, starting in 1978 and peaking in 2019, has turned sour. We have a new nationalism in the US that regrets most things global. And the main thing we regret is China.

Now, rather than celebrating my China roots and experience, I hide them. One of the few things that unites many aspects of American society is the belief that China is a problem. And not a little *p* problem, but an all-caps, exclamation-marked PROBLEM! According to Republican hawks such as Josh Hawley and Peter Navarro, China is a democracy-threatening, civilization-crushing security PROBLEM! According to Democrats such as Elizabeth Warren and Sherrod Brown, China is a labor-crushing, middle-class-gutting stooge of the corporate class used to smash the working man. PROBLEM! And for both sides, a guy like me who spent his career facilitating China engagement must surely have dubious intentions, a lack of patriotism, and a lack of loyalty. Not a China hand—a China heel.

A PROBLEM!

Even though I am deeply sympathetic to Taiwan, I do not support the China Evil Empire thesis. Not its blue-state version, nor its red-state version. I have known too many of China's people and worked with too many of its companies to be seduced by such humanity-erasing memeification. But there are legitimate issues we do need to discuss. Do the Chinese steal our intellectual property? Do Chinese state subsidies give Chinese businesses an unfair advantage? Have Chinese trade practices hollowed out the American middle class? Does the Chinese Communist Party have hostile intentions in the South China Sea? As I shall discuss, all these questions can be answered with both a yes and a no. It is important that we understand in what sense both these answers are possible at the same time.

However, the fact that the rise of China has severely impacted the United States is not subject to that same relativity. For sure, the rise of China has hit us like a tsunami.

But here's the emphatic point I will make: China's rise was not a Bond villain plot nor a capitalist betrayal of the working class. It was a historic, once-in-a-millennium disruptive occurrence, when one billion people suddenly joined the global marketplace. That is one-fifth of humanity who, in 1978, had been totally absent from that marketplace but who, in the span of twenty years, joined it more or less all at once.

Of course it was disruptive. How could it not be? It threw everything out of balance: capital, labor, trade, and our politics. But it was a disruption that was going to roll over us no matter what. China has always been a huge civilizational power. Its absence from that role over the last 150 years has been a strange historical anomaly. Like the railroad, like the internet, like AI today, there is no stopping that tsunami from rolling in. And like the railroad, like the internet, and like AI, trying to contain it, trying to reverse it, trying to cut it out of our lives is like trying to flatten that incoming tsunami with a wave of your hand. You just can't.

As I shall argue, China's rise was no one's genius, and neither was it anyone's fault. It was no one's explicit political intention, nor was it someone's economic misstep. It was something closer to physics, the weather, the simple tectonic movement of plates in the world of our geopolitics. All anyone could do was go where the winds and the waves were going to take them.

Some, like me, were on the right island at the right time and were able to ride it well; some, like my relatives in Ohio, very nearly drowned. Neither of us intended nor wished for any of that to happen. It just happened. And now that it has happened, it's not going to un-happen. There is only looking forward, rebuilding what is in our control to rebuild, and finding a way to make it work.

I am not a spokesperson for China, nor am I trying to be. I have lots of little *p* problems with China. I am not choosing China over my own country, even though I have many little *p* problems with the US. Truth be told, I want nothing more than for the US to maintain its (more or less) peaceful hegemony, that Pax Americana, that the country (and the world) has enjoyed since the end of World War II.

But like it or not, Pax Americana will also have to sit next to a Pax Sinica. Whether those two global orders integrate around their fringes and find a constructive way to do business or whether their borders are rimmed with outward-facing guns depends on the moves we make collectively in the near term.

To maintain the US's global strength and relevance and to engage China constructively, we must know a little something about the place we are confronting. Far too often, we are letting fringe political commentators, social media memes, and the blatantly uninformed frame the narrative for us. Our response to China will fail if we allow the nation to be framed as some monolithic abstraction, as an angry-face-emojied political meme, or as an Evil Empire. We need to remember that it is a living, breathing nation populated by 1.4 billion souls containing enormous diversity: ethnically, commercially, politically, ideologically.

I'm going to take a crack at showing you that living nation and the faces of its traders. First, I will examine a bit of US–China history and how each nation sees the other; then, I will analyze some of the "winners" and "losers" of our trade relationship; and then I will close by offering suggestions for how we best move forward together as the two largest economies on the planet.

My perspective will be different from most. In a time when readers and pundits will want to take sides in left/right, socialist/nationalist, or traitor/patriot, I'm going to take a middle path that tries to bring thoughtful, honest analysis to the full complexity of trade between these two global superpowers. Having a foot in both worlds is my natural stance. I am a third-culture kid, a global nomad, and my experiential reality is inhabiting that middle space *in between*. While that middle space may seem odd, even suspect, I believe I have been put here for a reason.

I get that you may not want to hear from a China heel. But I hope 125 years of my family's history in China, along with my own thirty years of heavily toiled China-handedness, will earn me at least your willingness to read a bit further and to consider, perhaps, a different perspective.

BRING
JOBS
HOME

NO
MORE
CHINA
TRADE

PART I

IS CHINA AN EVIL EMPIRE?

鸡同鸭讲

(Jī tóng yā jiǎng)

A conversation between chickens and ducks ...

BRING JOBS HOME
NO MORE CHINA TRADE

CHAPTER 1

THE CHINA AMERICA WANTED BUT DIDN'T GET

This is a book about US outsourcing. About tariffs, factories, container ships, and policy acronyms. But we can't start there. Because when it comes to the US–China relationship, trade is only one small part—the receipt, if you will—of an interaction that has spanned centuries.

If you read past the receipt, you realize that the history of that relationship is less about direct experience and more about storytelling. In other words, the US and China have rarely known one another—not in any sustained, intimate sense—and so what both sides possess are layers upon layers of delusions about the other. For most Americans, their "relationship" with China is not with China itself but with a story someone else—politicians, missionaries, journalists—has told them about China.

And stories, unlike receipts, don't add up neatly. They proliferate devoid of detail. They linger on vague emotions. They get passed down like folklore—like that child's game of telephone—and provide little help in conveying facts about the other side. As a result, when Americans talk about China, they are often, usually unconsciously, parroting other people's narratives. The actual lived reality of 1.4 billion people fades into nothingness, replaced by these incomplete narratives—rumors, sermons, think pieces, dinner table warnings—that may feel like truth only because they have been recirculated so many times.

Unfortunately, they are utterly unhelpful.

THE ABSENCE OF CONTACT

We like to think that US economic policies are clean, dispassionate, nation-blind, science-based decisions. But they are not. They are riddled with preferences, prejudices, and preconditions. And, for some reason, as I have come to experience it, the US–China trade relationship is particularly fraught with those prejudices: uniquely susceptible to overreaction, backlash, and confrontation. This is in contrast to our trade with, say, Japan, Thailand, or India—cultures equally distinct from ours but that manage to find a more dispassionate footing.

The reason for this is simple: While our trade with China is vast—$690 billion in goods exchanged in 2022[2]—it is handled almost exclusively through a relatively small number of intermediaries. Trading houses in Hong Kong, Western-educated factory owners in Taiwan, English-speaking investors in Southeast Asia, and, yes, a few former missionary kids like me. If your house is filled with goods made in China, chances are that you did not buy them at a market stall, haggling with a man from Shanghai, both of you testing the boundaries of price and trust, both of you having to reckon with the real human being in front of you. No—your toaster or lamp or pair of sneakers arrived shrink-wrapped on a Costco or Walmart shelf or by magic with a click of a computer mouse. Its price tag was not established by a conversation but by a contract handled three continents away.

Similarly, Chinese manufacturers sell to America without ever really knowing Americans. They negotiate with buyers in San Francisco, shipping brokers in Singapore, or sourcing agents in Shenzhen. They know the product specifications and the delivery schedules but not the people who will end up with the product in their homes. That's how our trade unfolds: Chinese sellers not knowing their ultimate buyer; American consumers buying from China without ever having to hear a word of Mandarin, to shake a hand calloused from factory work, or to see the face of the woman who stitched their jean jacket together.

In this way, our geopolitical "relationship" is devoid of any substance. We are bound by trade but without the intimacy of trade. By contrast, if you buy cheese from France, you might imagine the cow in Normandy, the village creamery, the Frenchman with an accent. If you buy olive oil from Italy, you picture the hillside groves and the village café. But with China, the images are blank: an anonymous factory, a faceless state, a label on a toy. This absence of direct contact leaves a vacuum, and vacuums do not remain empty for long. Into that space rush the tabloid storytelling, the prejudices, the narratives we inherit. You know, kung fu Orientalism, the communist monolith, the economic cheat.

Our geopolitical "relationship" is devoid of any substance. We are bound by trade but without the intimacy of trade.

For most Americans, China is a fictitious projection. And for most Chinese, America is just as much a fictitious projection. Our trading relationship is characterized by dueling ghoulish emanations—an MMA match of body-slamming ghosts.

It is an awful way to trade.

TODAY'S PROJECTED WINNER

And from this fog of projections, in the US, one storyline has muscled its way to the front. It drowns out the others because it is simple, emotional, and easy to chant on the campaign trail. It has the most airtime, the most moral punch, the most policy traction.

The current champion is this: **China is an Evil Empire.**

You might ask, Does anyone actually believe that? The answer is an emphatic yes—and not just a few people. The phrase itself is borrowed from Ronald Reagan's famous branding of the Soviet Union. Today, it has been revived—sometimes explicitly, sometimes in spirit—to describe China. Former Vice President Mike Pence warned in a 2023 Hudson Institute speech that "China may not yet be an evil empire—but it is working hard to become one."[3] The words are carefully hedged, but the moral framing is unmistakable: China is marching us all into the abyss.

Others dispense with the hedging. Speaking at a different Hudson Institute event, during a discussion titled "Seven Things You Can't Say About China," Senator Tom Cotton opened by bluntly saying, "China is an evil empire."[4] For him, it is neither a trajectory nor a risk but a settled fact. The Family Research Council wrote in late 2021, "China is now perhaps the main 'focus of evil in the modern world.' … We must now face down this threat and make sure that … we confront Beijing's evil and … see an end to yet another evil empire."[5] These are not fringe voices. These are voices from the mainstream of conservatism.

BEYOND THE RIGHT

Concern about China framed in moral or civilizational terms is by no means limited to conservatives. On the left, Senator Sherrod Brown championed legislation blocking Chinese solar panel makers from receiving US tax credits, arguing that "We cannot allow American tax dollars to go to Chinese companies that cheat and undermine American solar manufacturing."[6] The cheating to which he refers is Chinese state subsidies that support the nation's solar manufacturers.

But if subsidies alone make a country a cheater, then Germany must also be considered a cheater. In the 2000s, Germany became the undisputed global leader in solar manufacturing and installation, accounting for more than half of the world's installed solar capacity by 2010.[7] This dominance wasn't the product of laissez-faire competition. It was built on massive state subsidies through the Renewable Energy Sources Act, which guaranteed above-market feed-in tariffs for solar power—rates that reached €0.574 per kWh in 2004, nearly ten times the wholesale electricity price.[8] German firms such as Qcells and SolarWorld thrived in that environment, also supported by regional development grants and EU-backed financing totaling over €100 billion by 2015.[9]

Of course, China's solar subsidies have since dwarfed anything Germany attempted—Chinese government support reached an estimated $47 billion in 2022 alone.[10] And China's authoritarian style of governance adds complexity to its subsidies that may not exist with Germany. But that doesn't erase the fact that Germany's support was, for its time, extraordinary. Nor is Germany unique. The US oil and gas industry has enjoyed tax breaks, favorable leasing terms, and direct subsidies worth an estimated $20 billion annually over the past decade.[11] If every subsidy is cheating, then America's fossil fuel industry has been gaming the system longer than anyone. But we do not call Germany, and certainly not ourselves, cheaters.

Senator Elizabeth Warren has issued a warning about the Chinese Communist Party's (CCP) attempts to shape American industries through money and lobbying, raising alarms about the CCP's undue influence over US institutions.[12] What's notable is how singularly this charge is leveled against China. After all, the United Kingdom has long invested heavily in cultural diplomacy through institutions such as the British Council, spending £1.2 billion globally in 2022–2023,[13] and by funding chairs in British studies at American universities. No one accuses them of undermining US sovereignty despite the US having fought two wars with them. Likewise, France openly promotes its language and worldview through the Alliance Française network and subsidizes French film festivals across the United States. In none of these other cases do we brand the efforts as "undue influence." But, for some reason, when the solar subsidy comes from China or when the Confucius Institute is funded by China, everything is different.

It becomes evil.

NAMING THE GHOSTS

China is not an Evil Empire. It is large and influential—yes. Home to 1.4 billion people, the world's second-largest economy ($17.7 trillion GDP in 2023),[14] and a nuclear power with growing global reach. China is also diverse and far from monolithic: fifty-six recognized ethnic groups, vast regional differences in wealth and culture, and a population that includes everyone from tech entrepreneurs in Shenzhen to yak herders in Gansu. To frame China as an Evil Empire does nothing to help us understand how to work with one-fifth of humanity. What it reveals instead are the projections we've placed on it—projections that say more about America than about China.

And those projections are worth revisiting.

THE DEEP ROOTS OF OTHERING

My family has been working with China for 125 years. Four generations of us have lived there, worked there, studied there, preached there. We have helped form and circulate some of these very narratives, at times unwittingly. I know their staying power. And unless we name them for what they are—stories rather than facts—we will never make sense of the strange mixture of passion, suspicion, and policy overreaction that defines US–China relations today.

The reason so many Americans are drawn to the Evil Empire narrative isn't because they've studied Chinese governance and found it wanting. It's because that narrative feels familiar. It clicks into place with older stories we've been telling ourselves about China for centuries. These stories collide and compound, creating a kind of emotional momentum that sweeps up everything in its path: trade policy, military strategy, even mundane decisions about TikTok and solar panels.

At their core, these stories fall into three recurring arcs:

- China, the Economic Shangri-la
- China, a Land in Need of Saving
- China, the Great Disappointment

There are subnarratives that slot under each heading, but these three stories are the headliners. They are the ghosts that keep walking into the room just as the receipts of trade are being tallied. This analysis of American narratives is not an attempt to excuse or ignore the very real issues of human rights, military assertiveness, or economic policies within China today. Rather, it is an argument that we cannot hope to address those issues effectively until we first understand and clear away the historical fog of lazy, unchecked narratives.

Here we go ...

CHINA, THE ECONOMIC SHANGRI-LA

For centuries, Westerners have looked at China as something monumental. Here was a civilization older than Greece and Rome, one that had seemingly mastered wealth, order, and cosmic balance just as Europe was still wiping the snot off the face of the plague. The earliest Western accounts of China were filled with awe, even fantasy.

In the first century AD, Pliny the Elder complained that Rome was bleeding silver to pay for Chinese silk—so sheer, he said, that it made "our matrons look naked."[15] Emperor Tiberius tried to ban silk imports but failed; the demand was too strong. In the thirteenth century, Marco Polo sealed the legend, describing Kublai Khan's court as "so vast, so rich, and so beautiful, that no man on earth could design anything superior."[16] Polo may have exaggerated—historians debate whether he actually reached China—but the myth stuck: China was the place where roads were paved in stone, markets buzzed with every good under heaven, and wealth was endless if only you could reach it.

America's first corporation, the Virginia Company, chartered in 1606, explicitly sold investors on the fantasy that Jamestown might become a stepping stone to China. Not long after, the newborn United States wasted no time: In 1784, the merchant ship *Empress of China* sailed from New York to Canton, loaded with ginseng and silver. Fifteen months later, it returned with tea, porcelain, and silk—cargo worth $30,727, a 25 percent profit that ignited America's first China trade fever.[17] George Washington sipped tea from Chinese porcelain brought off that ship.

By the nineteenth century, "unlocking" the Chinese market had become an American obsession. Senator William Seward declared in 1869 that the Pacific, and beyond it, China, would be "the chief theater of events in the world's great hereafter."[18] America panted with expectation, intoxicated by the idea that China was both a prize and a promise: millions of souls to be converted; millions of customers to be won; and a vast, ancient civilization that could be an American prize instead of a European one.

Missionaries: By the mid-1800s, the American Board of Commissioners for Foreign Missions was funneling $200,000 annually into China, publishing pamphlets about the teeming millions waiting to be saved. Yale and Oberlin produced whole classes of missionaries who sailed across the Pacific with Bibles in hand, convinced China would be their crowning conversion.[19]

Merchants: New England's great fortunes—from Boston's Perkins family to New York's Astors—were rooted in the Canton trade. Ships carried ginseng, silver, and eventually opium, all justified by the dream that one day, if the doors swung open wide enough, China's four hundred million people could make a single American rich beyond measure. The Astor family alone made over $2 million from the China trade by 1850.[20]

Politicians: Senator Thomas Hart Benton argued in Congress that the United States was destined to be the "China power," dominating Pacific trade routes.[21] William Seward, Henry Clay, Thomas Benton—voices from both parties—echoed the same fixation: America's future ran through China.

Culture: The mania filtered into everyday life. American newspapers ran daily tea and silk prices from Canton as eagerly as they ran gold prices from California. Families in Salem, Providence, and Philadelphia displayed Chinese porcelain as symbols of sophistication.

Herman Melville, in *Moby-Dick* (1851), used Canton as shorthand for global commerce, writing of "the wealth of the Indies" flowing through its ports.[22]

Yet, for all the froth and fantasy, the "China trade" was mostly illusion. Americans devoured newspaper accounts, missionary letters, and novels about the Celestial Empire, but very few ever touched its shores. In 1869—the same year Seward was dreaming aloud—the United States had only a handful of vessels trading directly with China, largely controlled by Boston, New York, and Philadelphia firms. Meanwhile, British-flagged shipping dominated Far East routes with China-engaged ships numbering in the many hundreds, if not thousands, during the same era.* By the 1880s, fewer than one thousand Americans lived in China, almost all missionaries, and all stationed in treaty ports such as Shanghai and Canton.[23] By contrast, at the same time, there were seven thousand Americans living just in Paris.

For all the talk of unlocking the vast China market, the trade itself was narrow: tea, silk, and some manufactured goods trickling out of China; silver and specialty crops, such as ginseng, trickling in. China itself tightly restricted commerce, keeping foreigners confined to concessions and refusing to let them penetrate the countryside. The result was a strange gap: a country lionized as the world's greatest commercial prize yet engaged by only a tiny sliver of Americans, with the benefits flowing to even fewer. China was always that pot of gold at the end of the rainbow—within sight, but out of reach.

THE MODERN REVIVAL

Then, when Deng Xiaoping cracked open China's doors in the late 1970s, American CEOs believed their destiny had finally arrived. A billion people newly unleashed, newly hungry, and ready to buy. The numbers seemed to validate every historical fantasy. By 2010,

General Motors was selling more Buicks in China (550,000) than in the United States (180,000).[24] Starbucks opened a new café in China every fifteen hours at its peak expansion.[25] Apple generated $74 billion in revenue from China sales in 2021—nearly 20 percent of its total sales.[26]

By 2023, China's middle class numbered four hundred million, larger than the entire US population.[27] Its e-commerce market reached $1.8 trillion, bigger than America's and Europe's combined.[28] Its high-speed rail system stretched forty-five thousand kilometers—the distance from New York to LA multiplied by fifteen.[29] The math was always the same: Just capture 5 percent of this market, and we win big.

A lot of Americans, frustratingly, are still awaiting their wins.

CHINA, A LAND IN NEED OF SAVING

Alongside the view that China was a land offering vast riches sat another view, a moral view, that helped explain why those riches might be out of reach. It was a view born in the mid-nineteenth century, when China remained stubbornly indifferent to Western trade. Foreign merchants clamored for access; Chinese mandarins waved them away. The Qing court confined commerce, and even contact, to a corner of Canton and tolerated the Portuguese in Macau but little more.

This insouciance maddened Western powers, especially the British.

So, Britain forced open the door. Opium and naval gunboats achieved what diplomacy and trade missions could not. The First Opium War (1839–1842) ended with the Treaty of Nanjing, prying open five ports and ceding Hong Kong to the British. The Second Opium War (1856–1860) drove Chinese humiliation deeper, granting foreigners rights to travel inland, build churches, proselytize, import goods, and live under extraterritorial law rather than Chinese authority.

For China, these "unequal" treaties were not just political defeats but existential shocks. The Middle Kingdom—once self-styled as the center of the civilized world—was now carved up by island nations and forced into the role of student rather than teacher. The Qing dynasty hemorrhaged legitimacy; the Taiping Rebellion (a peasant led attempt to fight back Western encroachment) killed an estimated twenty to thirty million people between 1850 and 1864;[30] and by the century's end, China had sunk to its modern nadir.

It was precisely then that American missionaries arrived in force.

THE SECOND GREAT AWAKENING MEETS THE MIDDLE KINGDOM

Back home, the Second Great Awakening had swept across America, a tide of evangelical fervor democratic in spirit and uncompromising in mission. Its watchword was universal salvation, and its mandate—"Go ye into all the world"—resonated from Maine pulpits to Missouri camp meetings. Historian Andrew Preston has called it "the spiritual mobilization of American empire."[31] For many Americans, China seemed the ultimate test case: vast, ancient, pagan, and with four hundred million souls awaiting the gospel. If this land could be won for Christ, a massive chunk of humanity could be redeemed in a single sweep. The American Board of Commissioners for Foreign Missions thundered in 1850: "Let China be converted, and a third of the globe bows the knee to the Redeemer."[32]

By 1920, more than five thousand American missionaries lived and worked in China—far more than the American business and diplomatic population—supported by millions of Sunday school donations collected from Ohio to Kansas.[33] Mission presses churned out religious tracts. Their letters, pamphlets, and fundraising tours became the primary lens through which many ordinary Americans "knew" China. My own great-grandparents were part of this movement, stationed in Nanjing, writing home about the boys' school they ran, the hospital they built, the church they planted—and, of course, about the money they needed to keep it all alive.

In their private diaries, my great-grandparents expressed great love and admiration for China and a desire to spend their entire lives there. But fundraising requires urgency, and urgency requires emphasizing need. Without meaning to, the pamphlets they sent home painted China differently from their private letters—a bit more desperate, more lacking, more in need of rescue. They weren't being dishonest; they were doing what all fundraisers do: highlighting problems they were there to solve.

Yet, despite their deep and genuine love for China, they also believed China needed what America could provide. Supporters at home reading these appeals naturally absorbed that framing. This framing did two things at once. It humanized China for American audiences, replacing caricature with genuine compassion. But it also placed China inside a moral narrative whose endpoint had already been decided. With enough Christ-like labor, conversion was not merely hoped for; it was expected.

The result was that for vast swaths of the American public, China became synonymous with moral potential: A civilization not quite right by itself, but, oh, so very close, if only we keep shining our lights and showing the way.

This is not to comment on the purpose and efficacy of missionary work in general. I just mean to say this: The sheer size of the missionary population in China in the first third of the twentieth century and the huge volumes of tracts that circulated around the US about China created a deeply etched impression, however unconscious, that China was a land of enormous potential but in need of rescue—both economically and spiritually.

Even missionaries of the time acknowledged this. Henry W. Luce, a Presbyterian minister in Shandong and the father of *TIME* magazine's Henry R. Luce, worried that American churches were romanticizing China into a kind of moral project rather than as a real place. "The Chinese are not waiting for us to save them," he is often paraphrased as saying, "they are waiting for us to understand them."[34] Others, such as John Leighton Stuart—another Presbyterian minister, the president of Yenching University and later a US ambassador to China—feared that the missionary movement's vast publicity machine was teaching Americans to see China through a lens of dependency and destiny.

And—just to be clear—those missionaries did a tremendous amount of good, whatever it is you may have been taught in Anthropology 101. They brought medicine, education, printing presses, and new opportunities for women. Their schools seeded a generation of reformers who later helped build the Chinese Republic. By 1949, Protestant missions operated thirteen universities, more than two hundred middle schools, and more than six thousand primary schools in China.[35] Even Chinese skeptics of Christianity admitted their value. Reformer Liang Qichao observed in 1896 that while many Chinese remained wary of foreign religion, the missionaries' hospitals and schools had nonetheless introduced modern education and medicine to China, spreading learning and saving lives well beyond the church walls.[36]

THE GREAT EXPULSION AND LASTING WOUNDS

That's the heartbreak: American missionary support for China was sincere, well meaning, and far-reaching in its positive effects. So, when China eventually expelled all missionaries after 1949—branding them cultural imperialists and agents of Western subversion—the sting ran deep. The severing was not just political but personal for millions of

American congregations who had invested prayers, pennies, and their sons and daughters in China's salvation. By 1953, the last American missionaries had been expelled or imprisoned.[37]

That wound has never fully healed. Even today, evangelical organizations such as The Voice of the Martyrs or ChinaAid regularly update congregations on pastors arrested, underground churches raided, and Bibles confiscated. ChinaAid reports over ten thousand cases of religious persecution annually.[38] For many conservative Christians, these stories plug directly into one of the deepest narratives in Western Christian culture: forces of light under attack by forces of darkness.

FROM GOSPEL TO FREE MARKETS

While Christian conservatives still maintain the explicit missionary narrative, neoconservatives and liberals have developed their own version of it. For these neo-missionaries, the twentieth-century gospel became democracy and free markets. Ronald Reagan's Secretary of State, George Shultz, declared in 1985: "As people grow prosperous, they will demand participation. Freedom is the natural companion of markets."[39] The logic was missionary at its core: Teach China to trade, and political conversion would follow. Henry R. Luce, the missionary's son who built *TIME* magazine into America's voice of destiny, gave this faith its media catechism. In his 1941 essay "The American Century," Luce argued that the United States had a divine calling to remake the world in its image.[40]

This became mainstream Washington consensus across both parties. George Bush, arguing for China's World Trade Organization (WTO) entry in 2000, told Congress, "Trade freely with China and time is on our side. The more China liberalizes its economy, the more it will liberalize its politics."[41]

And as with Christianity a century earlier, there were real fruits. China embraced market reforms, grew rich, and joined the world system. But the deeper hope—that trade would turn China into "one of us"—proved elusive. When China failed to convert politically, the disappointment cut just as deeply as it had for Sunday school donors decades earlier. Senator Marco Rubio voiced this frustration in 2019: "For the last two decades, China fooled the world into believing it would accept a rules-based international order and become a responsible stakeholder … Instead, China … has tightened its one-party authoritarian rule …"[42]

Notice the phrase *fooled the world.* That implies a promise to change was explicitly made. For sure, China made no such promise. Instead, it was what some politician or think tank in Washington was promising about China.

Therein lies the rub.

This is the recurring theme of America's approach to China. Whether the mission is religious or secular, we do not merely trade with China; we want to transform it, improve it. We approach China not as customers approaching a supplier, or even as one sovereign nation engaging another, but as missionaries approaching potential converts. Whether the gospel is Christianity or democracy, the assumption remains the same: China needs what America can provide and providing it will fundamentally make China better.

Then, when China declines the altar call, America's disappointment becomes searingly bitter.

That is far too much existential angst for one trade relationship to bear.

CHINA, THE GREAT DISAPPOINTMENT

By the twentieth century, missionary zeal had mostly morphed into the modernization theory that access to markets would lead to democracy. US policy across parties and decades rested on that conviction: China would eventually, surely, become more like us. With enough exposure to American education, business, and institutions, China would "graduate" into a responsible stakeholder in the liberal order.

This was not an unreasonable expectation. The formula had worked before. Japan had emerged from feudalism and World War II devastation to become a democratic ally—GDP per capita rising from $391 in 1960 to over $39,000 by 2020.[43] South Korea had shed military dictatorship for vibrant democracy, with per capita income jumping from $158 in 1960 to $31,000 today.[44] Taiwan had transformed from authoritarian rule into a flourishing multiparty democracy. Each had followed a recognizable arc: economic development, middle-class growth, political liberalization, and eventual convergence with Western norms. The pattern seemed inevitable, almost scientific.

Why would China be different?

I remember arriving in Shanghai fresh out of college when Deng Xiaoping's reforms began rippling across the country. I'd hold court at the Long Bar in the Portman Hotel, telling anyone who would listen that I'd witnessed the political transformations in Taiwan in the late 1980s and that China was absolutely next. Around the same time, PBS's documentary series *The Pacific Century* framed Hong Kong not as a victim of China's return but as a harbinger of its future. One commentator captured the mood: "It's not so much that China is taking over Hong Kong, as Hong Kong taking over China."[45]

All of America—and much of the West—shared that electrifying expectation.

But China, in the end, was different. Way bigger than Japan or Korea, with ancient political instincts far more ingrained. Where other rising countries liberalized, China did not. Where others embraced imported institutions wholesale, China remodeled them for its own purposes. The trajectory looked familiar, but the hand on the tiller was unmistakably Chinese.

If the first American narrative was the fantasy of a golden prize waiting to be unlocked, and the second was the belief that, through missionary-like labor, China could be redeemed, then the third was disappointment. Because time and again, the Shangri-la, the conversion, the convergence just never came.

THE CYCLE OF BROKEN EXPECTATIONS

Disappointment keeps curdling into anger. China had not just failed to change; it had betrayed us. Cheated us. Deceived us. This was the rage of a spurned benefactor, the fury of a teacher whose star pupil had turned delinquent. Betrayal is not how you describe an adversary; it's how you describe a protégé who strayed.

The pattern of disappointment had been building for decades. In 1949, when Communist victory dashed American dreams, Secretary of State Dean Acheson declared that the US had "lost China."[46]

Decades later, Tiananmen Square crushed any hopes of political reform with melancholy finality. President George W. Bush addressed how he saw the image of students seeking freedom during his father's presidency as powerful, and that led him to want to believe that China had been becoming more like us, only to have those hopes dashed by the brutal crackdown.[47]

But American disappointment reached its apex with Xi Jinping. For a fleeting moment after Deng's reforms and China's WTO entry in 2001, it seemed that earlier letdowns might finally be undone.

Xi's rise shattered that illusion definitively.

He scrapped presidential term limits in 2018, making himself the most powerful leader since Mao. He dismantled fragile civil society spaces that had emerged during the reform era. He tightened censorship and surveillance into a digital panopticon, complete with "social credit" scoring affecting 1.4 billion people. In Hong Kong—once imagined by Westerners as the seed that would "take over China"—he imposed a National Security Law in 2020 that effectively ended the city's democratic aspirations.[48]

Because convergence had seemed so near, this disappointment cut deepest of all. Xi's defiance put a depressing finality to generations of American fantasies about China.

THE YEARNING FOR VINDICATION

Today, the chorus of disappointment remains loud and persistent. Political scientist David Shambaugh of George Washington University writes of China's "final phase" of rule characterized by growing institutional strain.[49] Gordon Chang has been predicting *The Coming Collapse of China* since 2001,[50] updating his timeline repeatedly as the collapse fails to materialize. More recently, strategist Peter Zeihan reassures Western audiences that China's demographic implosion and debt bubble mean inevitable collapse: "China's demographic crisis and industrial overcapacity mean it only has ten years left in its current trajectory."[51]

While their predictions may very well come true, it's hard not to notice a strange yearning embedded in this narrative: a desire for China to fail so America can be proven right, so the cycle of disappointment can close with vindication. It's a kind of secular conversion story: China's collapse as the just rewards for political sin, after which American-inspired redemption might begin anew.

We still await China's conversion.

There's only one problem with all this: Very few Chinese voices have been present in these narratives and projected fantasies. These visions are no more Chinese than Marco Polo's medieval dreams. China, in the end, was never waiting to be discovered, converted, or remade. It only desired to stand up again, to reclaim what it saw as its rightful place in the world. The Chinese have their own narratives—older than our republic, older even than the modern West itself. Every time we think we're writing China's story, we're at best scribbling commentary in the margins of a much older text.

We still await China's conversion.

And that's the bitterest disappointment of all: Not that China has failed to become us but that it was always becoming something else, borrowing what it needed from us while never intending to travel anything but its own road. We thought China was falling in love with us when in fact it was only studying the tools of romance to pursue the village girl back home.

Sure, we feel iced out. We hate that feeling.

But we can still trade.

CHAPTER 2

THE AMERICA CHINA WANTED BUT DIDN'T GET

So how does China see America?

The question itself is misleading. It assumes a single China and a single answer. Neither exists.

I learned this during a business trip to Suzhou in 2016. My company was evaluating where to locate a battery factory, and that morning I sat in a fluorescent-lit conference room with city officials who spoke in carefully rehearsed phrases about win-win cooperation and mutual respect. Their talking points could have been lifted directly from a *People's Daily* editorial. When I raised concerns about intellectual property—our product involved sensitive technology—one official smiled politely and replied, "There is no IP problem in China. That is an American story." The room fell quiet.

That evening, I had dinner with Mr. Liu, a factory owner who was to supply components for these batteries. Over hot pot and several rounds of baijiu, his tone could not have been more different. He asked about US investment visas and if I could introduce a lawyer. He wanted to know how to get his son into an American university.

He joked about Trump's tweets, which he read using a VPN. When I mentioned the morning's stiff government meeting, he waved his hand dismissively. "Those guys? They have to say that stuff. It's their job. But you and me? We're just trying to make money."

Same city. Same day. Two Chinas.

That contrast is not an anomaly; it is the key to understanding how China views the United States. And increasingly the two divergent views are merging into one.

Before we can make sense of China's perceptions of America, we need to understand a deep internal tension that has shaped Chinese society for centuries: The divide between what scholars often describe as the moral center and the economic periphery.

You could say the moral center in China is the government—but it is also more than the government. It is civil administration infused with moral authority. It is City Hall that also functions as the nearest equivalent to a Church: the place where politics, ideology, and moral direction converge. In China, administration and moral guidance have long been fused into the defining role of the central state.

From the Confucian censorate that monitored imperial officials to today's Central Commission for Discipline Inspection, the state has been understood as the guardian of order: rectifying disorder, purifying motives, and preserving harmony. Political legitimacy flows not from procedure or popular consent but from performance and moral credibility. When disorder rises, the instinct of the center is not to loosen control but to tighten it.

The economic periphery is something else entirely. It is the realm of local improvisation, personal networks, quiet rule-bending, and survival-driven pragmatism, the side of China that bends so the system does not break. Historically, it has included merchants working around imperial restrictions, peasants smuggling grain during famines, and factory owners skirting export rules to stay afloat. When the center becomes rigid, the periphery adapts. The two work with each other, and around each other, and ... sometimes against each other.

China's post-1978 rise did not come from ideological brilliance at the top. When I said in my introduction that China's rise was no one's genius, this is what I meant. This rise actually came from illegal experiments at the edges of society. In villages across Anhui and Sichuan, farmers quietly abandoned Mao-era collective farming and divided land into family plots. This was forbidden. But local cadres—hungry themselves—looked the other way. Grain yields rose. Famine receded. Only then did the Party bless the practice, rebranding it as the Household Responsibility System.

Deng Xiaoping did not design this revolution; he legalized it. His famous line "It doesn't matter whether a cat is black or white, as long as it catches mice" was less an ideology than an admission. The center ratified what the periphery had already proven to have worked.

This dynamic matters because it shaped how different parts of China came to see America.

TWO VIEWS OF AMERICA

For much of the reform era, China held two simultaneous—and contradictory—views of the United States.

At the periphery, America was an object of fascination. Factory owners, entrepreneurs, and provincial officials admired American wealth, technology, and openness. They wanted American customers and American know-how. They wanted their children educated in American universities and their companies embedded in global markets. Their admiration was practical and aspirational. America represented opportunity.

Yet it was a complicated admiration. I was often asked some version of the same question: How can a country so rich have so many homeless people? To many Chinese, America appeared wealthy but chaotic. Innovative but socially unstable. Freedom dazzled but was also lost. Nonetheless, however much of a spectacle it was, the US was still fascinating to behold.

The moral center saw something different. To Beijing, America was a warning: powerful and rich, yes, but also an unreliable hegemon. For years, this negative view was tempered by pragmatism. Whatever its flaws, America was useful. It offered markets, technology, and an international system China could learn to navigate. The center did not trust the US, but it needed it.

Just watching a night of TV in China you could see this split screen at work. A hyped NBA expo game in Shanghai with beaming young people lined up for autographs, broadcast right before a news program explaining American hegemonic military interventions in the Middle East.

These days, thanks almost entirely to the trade war, the balance has tipped in favor of the government view.

As US–China relations deteriorated—through the Obama administration's pivot to Asia, Trump's first trade war, Biden's technology restrictions, and now a bipartisan turn toward confronting an "Evil Empire"—the economic periphery has begun to reassess its assumptions. The arguments once dismissed as propaganda—that America would never accept China's rise—started to feel plausible.

Mr. Liu told me this directly during a frustrated video call in 2023. "They always said America wouldn't let us succeed," he said. "I didn't believe it. I thought if we followed the rules, they'd accept us. But look—we built Huawei into the best telecom company in the world, and they banned it. We made better electric cars, and they raised tariffs. They don't want competition. They want us to stay poor."

This shift is significant. The moral center, sensing a new realignment with its periphery, has moved quickly to consolidate mutual commiseration. The narratives it had long promoted, once tolerated as background noise by entrepreneurs like Mr. Liu, now feel confirmed by events.

The three stories that the central government has told for a long time are increasingly the stories being shared among the economic periphery. They are:

- Never Again: China's defensive nationalism
- The United States: Hypocritical Hegemon
- The East Is Rising; the West Is Declining

These narratives now work together, reinforcing one another. And they did not emerge from trade disputes alone. They are rooted in history, grievance, and perceived betrayal. The trade war is just the latest round of evidence that proves the historical grievance must have been true all along.

NEVER AGAIN: CHINA'S DEFENSIVE NATIONALISM

On countless evenings during my years in China, I returned from factory visits to anonymous provincial hotels, usually after a big factory dinner, and flipped on China Central Television. What often greeted me were lavish historical dramas—*The Founding of a Republic* (2009), *The Hundred Regiments Offensive* (2015)—slick, well-funded productions with a single, unmistakable message: China had been humiliated by foreign powers, and the Communist Party had reversed that humiliation.

The pattern rarely varied. Foreign soldiers burned villages. Western diplomats sneered at Chinese officials. Opium merchants prowled treaty ports. Then discipline arrived. The Party entered the story, incorruptible and resolute. The closing scenes would feature the red flag rising, Mao declaring that "the Chinese people have stood up," crowds roaring as a century of shame came to an end.

These dramas gushed out the message that the moral center wanted its people to hear. Without the Party, China was weak (and would again be weak); with the Party, China would never again be humiliated.

This narrative draws its power from what Chinese historians call the Century of Humiliation: the period from the First Opium War in 1839 to the founding of the People's Republic in 1949. Every Chinese student learns this chronology: the Opium Wars, the burning of the Summer Palace, the carving up of treaty ports, the Japanese invasion, the Nanjing Massacre. The lessons are consistent and rehearsed. Weakness invites predation. Foreign powers exploit vulnerability. Sovereignty is never given; it must be defended.

This memory is continuously rehearsed through textbooks, museum exhibits, television dramas, and anniversary marches. To grow up in China is to inherit this sense of grievance, and to absorb a national vow: never again.

Xi Jinping gave this vow its clearest expression at the Party's centennial celebration in 2021: "The time in which the Chinese nation could be bullied and abused by others is gone forever." He warned, "Anyone who would attempt to do so will find themselves on a collision course with a great wall of steel forged by over 1.4 billion Chinese people."[52] This language frames Chinese policy—economic, diplomatic, and military—as fundamentally defensive. From Beijing's perspective, military strength is insurance not aggression. Control is not tyranny; it is stability preserved before chaos can return.

WHY COMMUNISM STILL STANDS

This helps explain something that often puzzles American observers: the enduring legitimacy of communism in China.

In the Western tradition, legitimacy rests on rights and consent. Government exists to restrain power. Chinese political thought evolved in the opposite direction. From Confucius to Mencius, legitimacy was performance-based. Rulers were expected to maintain order, prevent famine, and keep harmony. When they failed, rebellion was justified.

Communism resonated in China less as ideology than as a delivery mechanism. When Mao's forces came to power, what mattered to peasants was not Marxist theory but land reform, grain distribution, and stability. As one oft-told story from the early 1950s goes, a farmer in Henan received the deed to land his family had farmed for generations as tenants. Holding the paper, he reportedly said, "My father died a renter. I will die an owner." It was collective ownership, of course, under the leadership of the Party, but that was better than being a serf under one greedy landlord.

In its early decades, Communist rule in China did deliver on its promise. Between 1952 and 1978, official data shows average annual GDP growth above 6 percent, with industrial output rising by more than 120 percent during the First Five-Year Plan alone.[53] National income and literacy improved, life expectancy lengthened, and a modern industrial base was built virtually from nothing. China was poor, but it was progressing.

Then came the turn away from Mencius and toward Marx alone. Ideological purity began to outweigh human judgment. The Great Leap Forward (1958–1962) killed an estimated fifteen to forty-five million people, and the Cultural Revolution (1966–1976) tried to erase "old customs, old culture, old habits, old ideas,"[54] turning children against parents and severing ancient lineages. By the late

1970s, the verdict was clear: Marx without Mencius had nearly destroyed China. The Party's survival required grafting socialism back onto Chinese tradition.

Cue the farmers of Anhui and Sichuan. Cue Deng's pragmatic opening up. Cue the reassertion of the entrepreneurial periphery that was finally permitted to help the state feed the people. Out of this came a new fusion of Marx and Mencius that still defines Beijing's logic today: *socialism with Chinese characteristics*. From Mencius comes the moral duty to enrich the people and preserve harmony, whatever it takes. From Marx—channeled through Lenin—comes the machinery of state power to ensure that promise is delivered. The result is a system that justifies control not as tyranny but as guardianship: Stability first, prosperity next, liberty later—if ever.

When Beijing spends tens of billions on electric vehicles (EVs) and solar panels, helping China control approximately 80 percent of solar manufacturing stages,[55] Western critics cry "market distortion" or argue that these investments break WTO rules. From Beijing's perspective, supporting domestic industries—whether batteries, steel, or shipbuilding—is more about giving the nation something to grow around. This is in line with Chinese instincts on rulership for thousands of years. It is the modern iteration of the ancient granary system: government leadership (with overt intervention if needed) to ensure growth, prosperity, technological independence, and social stability.

Whether we agree or not with this framing, the Party's economic record provides powerful internal validation. Since 1980, China has lifted over eight hundred million people from poverty[56]—the largest shift out of poverty in human history. The GDP per capita rose from $195 in 1980 to over $12,000 by 2021.[57] Life expectancy has increased from sixty-six years in 1980 to seventy-seven years today.[58]

This success reinforces China's conviction that its Chinese brand of communism works. Party leaders also believe that its opposite—American-style democracy—will bring Chinese collapse. Xi Jinping said it plainly in 2013: "Copying Western political systems could lead to disaster for China."[59] The Soviet collapse only hardened this view. When the USSR disintegrated in 1991, Russian GDP collapsed 40 percent in the 1990s while oligarchs looted state assets.[60]

China is increasingly confident in its view of the world. Which is why American human rights pressure collides with China's own sense of moral self-understanding. When American officials insist they will "never stop pressing for human rights," Beijing hears a demand that China's moral tradition—thousands of years old—must yield to a foreign one. To them, it sounds like the old missionary reflex returning under a new banner.

I saw hints of this during my years in Chinese factories. American buyers would arrive with compliance questionnaires: *Do you employ children? Do you pay fair wages?* One export manager in Ningbo finally snapped, "Can we send you a questionnaire asking how many schoolchildren were shot in your city this year? Maybe *we* don't want to sell to *you*." His anger wasn't about the form. It was about being morally lectured by people who knew nothing of his world.

Technology restrictions confirm these biases in the minds of most Chinese. When National Security Advisor Jake Sullivan defended semiconductor export controls by saying America must "maintain as large of a lead as possible" over China,[61] Washington saw it as a reasonable and prudent national security initiative. Beijing saw confirmation that the West intends to cap China's rise, to treat it as a perpetual apprentice whose ingenuity must be monitored and managed.

China collectively says, "Never again."

THE UNITED STATES: HYPOCRITICAL HEGEMON

After the prime-time historical dramas rolled their credits, then came the late night talking-head forums. If the dramas were about reversing humiliation, the expert panels were about the untrustworthy Americans. Night after night, Chinese scholars, former diplomats, and military analysts dissected American foreign policy with prosecutorial zeal. Picture polished sets, authoritative voices, PowerPoint slides filled with dates and statistics. The conclusion rarely varied: America says one thing and does another.

A trade expert explains how America championed free markets until China started winning. A security analyst lists US military interventions. A former ambassador details how Washington designed international institutions, then ignored the rulings when they proved inconvenient. The message is clear: This is not a reliable partner but a hegemon that changes rules to maintain dominance.

For decades, American leaders urged China to embrace free trade. Treasury Secretary Robert Rubin said in 1999, "We believe it [WTO entry] has to be done on a basis that represents real market opening in China … just as open markets have been very good for our United States and countries around the world. …"[62] But when China's exports surged—reaching a $419 billion trade surplus with the US by 2018[63]—Washington rediscovered protectionism. The 2018 trade war slapped duties on more than $350 billion of Chinese goods.[64] President Trump declared, "Trade wars are good, and easy to win."[65]

The same contradiction appeared regarding technology. Washington praised competition and innovation as American strengths until Huawei gained ground in 5G and TikTok captured 170 million American users.[66] Suddenly, the rhetoric shifted to national security threats and outright bans. To Americans, these were prudent safeguards against authoritarian surveillance. To Beijing, they proved America believes in free markets only until a Chinese firm starts capturing market share.

America's perceived hypocrisy extends far beyond economics. When US officials lecture Beijing about respecting sovereignty in the South China Sea, Chinese diplomats reach for a well-stocked counter-arsenal: Iraq was invaded without UN approval in 2003; the humanitarian mission in Libya morphed into regime change in 2011; America occupied Afghanistan for twenty years before a chaotic withdrawal; the United States maintains roughly 750–800 base sites in about eighty countries.[67]

Chinese officials frequently cite these examples when defending their own policies. When Washington criticizes Beijing's economic coercion of countries such as Australia or Lithuania, Chinese diplomats respond with lists of American sanctions on Cuba, Iran, Russia, and dozens of other nations. The implicit message: If America can use economic pressure to advance its interests, why can't China?

Consider the WTO dispute system. America championed binding arbitration when it helped pry open foreign markets. But when WTO panels ruled against US steel tariffs, agricultural subsidies, or "Buy American" provisions, Washington balked. The Trump administration blocked the appointment of new WTO appellate judges until the system effectively collapsed.[68] Beijing's interpretation: America designed international law as a tool for others to follow, not as rules for the US to obey.

The dollar's role provides another example. Washington leverages the greenback's reserve currency status to impose unilateral sanctions that punish third-party countries for trading with American adversaries. European companies have faced billions in fines for doing business with Iran, even when their governments opposed US sanctions.[69]

From Beijing's perspective, this represents the US weaponization of economic interdependence while preaching free trade.

For Chinese elites who came of age during reform, the charge carries special sting. Many who studied in American universities, worked for American companies, or believed in economic convergence expected that integration would lead to mutual respect. The trade war felt like betrayal: America invited China into the global economy, then changed the rules when China succeeded.

This hypocritical hegemonic narrative legitimizes China's push to construct parallel institutions. The Belt and Road Initiative's $1 trillion in planned investment across more than 140 countries[70] is framed not as expansionism but as providing alternatives to Western-dominated development finance. Cross-border payment systems such as the Clearing House Interbank Payments System aim to reduce reliance on the Society for Worldwide Interbank Financial Telecommunication (SWIFT). Digital yuan trials explore how a sovereign digital currency might bypass dollar-dominated financial plumbing. The logic is insurance, not replacement: It needs the ability to turn elsewhere if American pressure becomes unbearable.

Back in Suzhou, this narrative shapes how Chinese citizens such as Mr. Liu interpret American actions. When Washington restricts Chinese students in STEM programs or delays visas, the citizens don't see security measures; they see confirmation that America never intended to welcome Chinese success. While Americans understand that such policies are the vagaries of this current administration, and that they are the harshest they've been in modern memory, such nuance does not make it to the Chinese family dinner table. To Mr. Liu, it feels like an American nationwide attack on the Chinese people. Now, instead of Stanford, he's hoping his son will study in the UK.

Of course, Beijing's ledger is selective. It downplays its island building in the South China Sea, its coercive trade measures against smaller states, and its own uses of extraterritorial pressure. But selectivity is the point. To a people the government knows is fascinated by the spectacle that is the United States, it says, "Look away—you are not invited to America's party. Just come home for dinner. I'll wait up."

THE EAST IS RISING; THE WEST IS DECLINING

On certain Saturdays during my years in China, the TV glowed with magnificent variety shows—hours of choreographed patriotism, songs about the Chinese dream, children in sequined costumes waving red flags. It was Broadway with Mandarin characteristics: jubilant, polished, watched by hundreds of millions. And the extravaganza's message was unmistakable: "The East is rising."

Then there was a flip to a Chinese news program, like *Xinwen Lianbo*. The neon vanished; senior officials spoke calmly about "the West in decline." I felt the dissonance—China's rise framed as inevitable, my own civilization narrated nightly as exhausted and in retreat.

If hypocrisy explains how Beijing reads America, China thinks time will do most of the hard work. Xi Jinping told the Party's Central Committee in 2017: "The world is undergoing profound changes unseen in a century. Time and momentum are on our side."[71] In 2021, Xi sharpened the message: "The East is rising, and the West is declining. This is not a short-term phenomenon, but a long-term trend."[72]

Beijing looks at the data and sees confirmation. China's share of global GDP has risen from less than 2 percent in 1980 to nearly 18 percent today.[73] It is the world's largest trading nation ($6.9 trillion in 2022)[74] and the world's largest manufacturer (28 percent of global output),[75] and it holds the largest foreign exchange reserves (approximately $3.2 trillion).[76] While America spent two decades and over $2 trillion bogged down in Middle Eastern wars,[77] China became the world's factory floor. In 2024, China bought approximately thirty-one million vehicles, more than the US and Europe combined.[78] It built more renewable energy capacity in 2022 alone than most countries possess in total and processes approximately 85 percent of rare earth elements.[79]

State media contrasts these figures with images of American dysfunction. Government shutdowns, infrastructure collapse, and power grids failing during storms. The January 6 attack on the US Capitol became a recurring exhibit: Democracy eating itself on live television. COVID-19 delivered an even starker lesson: America politicized basic public health measures and recorded more than one million deaths, a figure that shocked Chinese observers.[80]

As one *Global Times* op-ed put it: "The beacon of democracy now flickers in chaos. Why should China take lessons from a fading light?"[81]

The 2008 financial crisis occupies a special place in this narrative. For decades, American banks and regulators lectured the world on market discipline, until Wall Street required massive taxpayer bailouts. To many Chinese economists and policymakers, this confirmed what they already suspected: Western capitalism preached virtue but practiced excess. Premier Li Keqiang captured the sentiment in 2015: "Western countries borrowed from the future to pay for today. China invests in the future to build tomorrow."[82] (Of course, this is ignoring China's own debt problems.)

China projects itself as disciplined, patient, and future focused. When American politicians struggle to fund basic maintenance, China unveils trillion-dollar infrastructure plans. When US companies obsess over quarterly earnings, Chinese firms think in five-year cycles.

The Party frames current developments as the great rejuvenation of the Chinese nation. Not a new power, but a very old power returning to centrality.

This civilizational perspective shapes how Beijing interprets setbacks. Trade wars, technology restrictions, and diplomatic pressure are viewed as desperate attempts by a declining hegemon to slow China's inevitable rise. Xi told Party cadres in 2019 that the world was in turmoil, but he stated his belief that China had reason for strategic confidence, citing its long history, strong culture, and the momentum of rejuvenation.

IGNORING THE HEADWINDS

Yet, the confidence being sung and danced into existence carries risk. The Chinese narrative of ascendency collides with some inconvenient realities. China's population peaked in 2022 and is now shrinking—the first decline in six decades.[83] By 2035, China will have more people over sixty than the entire US population.[84] Total debt reached approximately 295 percent of GDP by 2023[85]—higher than US ratios before the 2008 crisis. Youth unemployment hit record highs above 20 percent before authorities stopped publishing the data.[86] Foreign direct investment fell 8 percent in 2023 as companies diversified supply chains away from China.[87]

None of these problems fits neatly into the "East is rising" storyline, creating dissonance that Beijing manages by doubling down on confidence. Official commentary admits challenges but frames them as growing pains, temporary turbulence on a long upward rise. Because, of course, admitting serious weakness would puncture the story that legitimizes Party rule.

The result is a dangerous geopolitical equilibrium. Each side believes the other's decline is inevitable. Each believes their own ascent is assured. Each interprets pressure as proof of the other's weakness. And when two nuclear-armed powers both conclude that history is on their side, patience becomes provocation and compromise looks like surrender.

Taken together, these three narratives—Never Again, Hypocritical Hegemon, and The East Is Rising; the West Is Declining—form the core of China's worldview. For Beijing, disputes are never just about soybeans or semiconductors—they're about humiliation avoided, hypocrisy exposed, and the long arc of history endured. Each negotiation becomes a test of whether China will again submit to foreign pressure or finally claim its rightful place as a great power.

For Beijing, disputes are never just about soybeans or semiconductors—they're about humiliation avoided, hypocrisy exposed, and the long arc of history endured.

China had once hoped for a very different America: a partner it could trust; one that would treat China with the respect owed to an ancient civilization; and one that would embrace the win-win ethos promised by globalization and free trade. What it believes it has received instead is a hegemon intent on maintaining its dominance, a hypocrite that preaches rules but breaks them when inconvenient, and—most painfully—a fresh round of humiliation to layer atop the century it has already never forgotten.

This creates a vicious cycle. Two superpowers, animated by opposing, hardening narratives, now face each other with nuclear weapons.

What is a cross-cultural businessman to do?

In-betweenists like me, who have lived on both sides, know that neither story is fully true, and that both contain enough truth to be dangerous. I understand why China believes what it believes. I understand why Americans believe what they believe. It's impossible for me to choose a side.

To live across these two cultures is to watch your two worlds slowly drift apart, and then, suddenly, to realize you are watching them divorce on live television. Each side tells its own story. Each is convinced of its innocence. And the middle space, where translation once happened, grows narrower by the day.

Unfortunately for me, history has never been kind to those who tried to stand between two hardening certainties.

BRING
JOBS
HOME
NO
MORE
CHINA
TRADE

CHAPTER 3

THIS JOHN SERVICE MOMENT

Let me tell you two stories: one personal, one national.

The first is small but close to home. A relative of mine—deep into MAGA politics—recently started posting clips on Facebook from a conservative commentator named Matt Walsh. In one video, Walsh warns that China has become an Evil Empire bent on crushing Christianity. Beginning May 1, 2025, he claims, foreign missionaries will be banned from preaching without government approval, with only state-sanctioned sermons allowed. Preach the wrong thing, he says, and you disappear.[88]

So far, so predictable. But then, Walsh takes a sharp turn. Suddenly, he's talking about Australia, declaring that Down Under it is now illegal to pray over someone questioning their gender identity, even if they ask for it. China's aggressive stance against Christianity has somehow caused liberals in Australia to act boldly. He concludes, "Authoritarian regimes—whether in Beijing or Sydney—understand something too many in the West have forgotten: Faith is a threat to their power. We thought we were going to change China. But what really happened is that China changed us."[89]

My relative shares this as proof that free trade didn't liberalize China but instead corrupted the West. What this relative doesn't do—what he has never done—is ask me what I think. He knows my history. He knows I lived in China for decades, built businesses there, raised a family there. Yet, in his mind, that very experience makes me suspect. Too much sympathy for the enemy. Too much contamination by proximity.

His unwillingness to engage directly speaks volumes. He illustrates how deeply warped our conversation about China has become. Somehow, at least in MAGA circles, even Australia's transgender policies get laid at Beijing's feet. In these projections, China stops being a real place and becomes a symbolic villain: An all-purpose answer to every anxiety about modern life.

Which brings me to my second story.

If my relative's Facebook feed is the grassroots version of this distortion, the fight over Intel's new CEO, Lip-Bu Tan, is the elite version. Tan's life is a classic American success story with a global twist. Born in Malaysia and educated in Singapore and California and at MIT, he built a career connecting Silicon Valley's ideas with Asia's engineering talent. Later, as CEO of Cadence Design Systems, he helped bridge the divide between American chip designers and Asian manufacturers.

But now, in Washington, those very bridges are being cast as threats. In August 2025, Senator Tom Cotton sent a letter questioning whether Tan's past investments in Chinese tech firms—including some allegedly linked to the military—posed a national security risk. Days later, Donald Trump called for Tan's resignation, branding him highly conflicted. Adding fuel to the fire, Cadence—Tan's former company—acknowledged selling chip design software to a Chinese military university, though it was in no way clear this was any threat to the US.

The timing couldn't be worse. Intel is supposed to be the crown jewel of America's effort to rebuild domestic chipmaking, powered by billions in CHIPS and Science Act subsidies. Yet one of its leaders is now portrayed as compromised, even dangerous, simply because he has spent his career moving between the US and China. Yet, perhaps incongruously or perhaps as a mechanism to leverage control, in August of 2025, Trump announced his intention that the US government purchase a 10 percent stake in Intel.

I don't know, but to me, this all feels like McCarthyism 2.0.

Which brings me to a man named John Service, an American diplomat serving in China in the mid-twentieth century.

If the first two chapters explored the stories Americans and Chinese tell about each other, this chapter asks what happens when those stories collide with reality. What happens when Americans must confront the China that exists, not the one we imagine or conjure?

Today, as the United States contends with a rising China under Xi Jinping's authoritarian rule, we face what I call a John Service Moment. John Service is a name Americans would be wise to remember. Most have never learned it. Studying John Service, we are better equipped to face critical options in how the US views China. We can engage with China as it is, accepting the messy compromises engagement requires. Or we can cling to illusions about what we wish China would become—and pay the price in failed policies, missed opportunities, and, very likely, lost lives. The question before us isn't whether we like China's system. It's whether we can build policy around Chinese realities and work with them constructively.

The question before us isn't whether we like China's system. It's whether we can build policy around Chinese realities and work with them constructively.

Service's story matters because today's moment echoes 1949 and 1950, when America was suddenly forced to confront a China very different from the one Washington had imagined. How we responded then shaped the next half-century of Asia policy, defined more by war and conflict than by understanding. Most of all, how we treated those issuing early warnings should inform how we listen and act today.

John Service was right. And I'll tell you why.

A TRUE THIRD-CULTURE KID

John Service was born in 1909 in Chengdu, Sichuan province, to YMCA missionaries.[90] His father worked to modernize Chinese agriculture; his mother taught in mission schools. Growing up speaking the local dialect and playing with Chinese children, Service moved easily between two worlds—one Chinese, one American—a feature that would define his life.

After graduating Phi Beta Kappa from Berkeley in 1931, Service felt like a foreigner in America and longed to return to China. Joining the Foreign Service in 1933, he was quickly posted to Beijing. Unlike most diplomats, who required years of training, Service was already fluent in Mandarin and attuned to unspoken cues. This gave him something rare in Washington: a reality gauge. While others relied on ideology or sanitized reports about a China that was supposed to be our ally, he described what he actually saw: collapsing villages, corrupt warlords, and soldiers who looked fierce on parade but fled in battle.[91]

THE MISSION TO YAN'AN

By the late 1930s, China was split between two rival governments. The Nationalists, the official party ruling China, were led by Chiang

Kai-shek and were America's allies and recipients of US aid. The problem was their military performance was poor.[92] General Joseph "Vinegar Joe" Stilwell warned that Chiang's army was "a hollow shell," hoarding American supplies for a future civil war instead of fighting Japan.[93] Japan had invaded Manchuria in 1931.

Reports suggested that the Nationalists' rival Communist forces were waging effective guerrilla campaigns against the Japanese. These fighters operated as a sort of second Chinese government, running schools, collecting taxes, and providing basic justice and order in the countryside while the Nationalists focused on the cities. Their presence was a mystery to most Americans, who only heard Nationalist propaganda portraying the Communists as bandits or Soviet puppets. To cut through the myths and assess these fighters, the US military sent the first official delegation to Communist territory: the Dixie Mission. Stilwell selected members for their analytical skill, and Service was a natural choice.

Arriving in Yan'an in July 1944, Service found not a sinister revolutionary fortress but a disciplined center of governance carved into northern hills. Though people were poor, morale was high.[94] In a three-hour meeting, the communist leader, Mao Zedong, impressed Service as pragmatic and focused on China's future.[95] Local governance surprised him with open meetings and village elections. Compared to Nationalist areas, Communist zones felt less authoritarian and more participatory.[96] Most crucially, the Communists had genuine popular support. Peasants backed them because taxes were fair, land reform real, and soldiers disciplined. On August 9, 1944, Service cabled Washington: "The Communists are in China to stay. And China's destiny is not Chiang's but theirs."[97]

It was a prescient warning built on observation, not ideology. But Washington hated the sound of it: Chiang was supposed to be the democratic reformer, and US aid was supposed to be building a reliable ally. Service's truth-telling disrupted that narrative—and for that, he would pay dearly.

THE PRICE OF TRUTH

Trouble began almost immediately upon Service's return to Beijing. In 1945, the FBI raided *Amerasia*, a left-leaning magazine, and discovered that Service had shared background information out of frustration at being ignored.[98] In the anticommunist climate, any link to suspected leftists looked like treason. He was arrested but never indicted. The FBI admitted there was no real case.

The real persecution began with Senator Joseph McCarthy. In February 1950, McCarthy claimed that the State Department harbored hundreds of communists, naming Service among them.[99] He accused Service of deliberately sabotaging US interests with his reports from Yan'an.[100] These attacks were amplified by the powerful China Lobby, including *TIME* publisher Henry R. Luce, the missionary's son discussed earlier, who vilified Service and others who criticized Chiang's regime—a regime Luce poured many tons of ink into promoting to the American public.[101]

Over five years, Service endured investigations, hearings, and public smears. Though never convicted of a crime, his career was destroyed. His family suffered; his children were sent to boarding school overseas to escape harassment, while his marriage was strained to the breaking point.

VINDICATION AND REHABILITATION

The vindication of John Service began slowly in the late 1950s as the worst excesses of McCarthyism were exposed. In 1957, the Supreme

Court ruled in *Service v. Dulles* that Service's dismissal from the State Department had been unlawful, and he was reinstated with back pay.[102]

More importantly, history proved Service's analysis correct. The Communists defeated the Nationalists in 1949, exactly as Service had predicted. Academic vindication followed. John King Fairbank, the dean of American China studies at Harvard, wrote in 1972, "John Service's reporting from Communist China in 1944 was the most accurate and insightful political analysis produced by any American diplomat in the twentieth century."[103]

Perhaps the most significant vindication came from Richard Nixon himself. When Nixon announced the opening to China in 1971, he was essentially implementing the policy Service had recommended twenty-seven years earlier. Henry Kissinger later acknowledged, "Had we followed John Service's advice in 1944, we might have avoided two decades of mutual hostility and the enormous costs of the Korean War."[104]

In the Korean War alone, American losses hit over thirty-six thousand. But the losses from broken communication, of course, extended far beyond the Korean War. Diplomatic isolation from China contributed to the escalation of the Vietnam War as policymakers misread Chinese intentions and capabilities. Meanwhile, China's isolation from moderating Western voices may have worsened the human catastrophes of the Great Leap Forward and Cultural Revolution. During those dark periods—when millions died from famine and political persecution—there were no American diplomats in Beijing to quietly counsel restraint, no cultural exchanges to remind Chinese leaders of alternatives to revolutionary extremism, no ongoing dialogue that might have provided face-saving ways to moderate disastrous policies.

THIS SERVICE MOMENT

Today, as America grapples with the rise of China, we face the same fundamental choice Service confronted. Like Service's Washington superiors in the 1940s, today's policymakers often favor intelligence that confirms their preconceptions rather than challenges them. Senator Marsha Blackburn once tweeted, "China has a 5,000 year history of cheating and stealing. Some things will never change . . ."[105] Senator Marco Rubio claimed that China had "cheated its way to superpower status."[106] These sweeping declarations dismiss China's economic and technological achievements as nothing more than deceit rather than the product of scale, strategy, and decades of deliberate national planning.

> **Like Service's Washington superiors in the 1940s, today's policymakers often favor intelligence that confirms their preconceptions rather than challenges them.**

If Service were alive today, observing Xi Jinping's China with the same clear eyes he once turned on Mao's movement, what would he tell Washington? I believe his views would include the following.

CHINA IS NOT GOING AWAY

Service would recognize that Xi's China, like Mao's in 1944, is here to stay. He would acknowledge its genuine achievements—poverty reduction, infrastructure development, technological advancement—alongside its authoritarian excesses. He would warn that China's system, however distasteful to American values, enjoys substantial domestic support and has demonstrated remarkable resilience.

America's choice, he would argue, is not between engaging with a China we like versus one we don't. It's between engaging with the China that exists or failing to influence it at all.

START WITH FACTS—AND FACE THEM HONESTLY

Service was an old-fashioned fieldworker who believed accurate analysis required direct observation. While many American diplomats in the 1940s stayed inside the foreign concessions or spoke only with Nationalist officials, he sat on rough benches in Yan'an, ate millet with peasants, and asked questions that few in Washington even knew to ask. His dispatches from China were almost works of anthropology. But gathering facts was only half the challenge. The harder part was forcing Washington to confront those facts when they didn't fit its preferred narrative.

DISTINGUISH BETWEEN IDEOLOGY AND NATIONAL INTEREST

US politicians, diplomats, and policymakers read Mao's speeches and saw nothing but Marxism. Service read the same words and saw something subtler: a nationalist movement using Marxist language to fundamentally pursue the Chinese goals of sovereignty, territorial integrity, and modernization. These were the same aims Chinese reformers had sought since the Opium Wars.

He warned that treating Mao as merely an extension of Moscow would distort US strategy. Mao's CCP was pragmatic and nationalistic. Its focus was on defeating Japan, overthrowing the corrupt Nationalists, and rebuilding China, not exporting revolution.

History proved Service right. After their 1949 victory, the Communists turned inward to rebuild their country. And when the

Sino-Soviet split erupted in the 1960s, it confirmed Service's insight: China's national interests would always outweigh ideological solidarity.

ENGAGEMENT BEATS ISOLATION

Service consistently argued for diplomatic recognition and direct dialogue with the CCP government. He understood that diplomacy wasn't endorsement. Two decades later, when Nixon shook hands with Zhou Enlai, he opened a door that had been needlessly shut for a generation. That single act reshaped the Cold War, isolated the Soviet Union, and began integrating China into the global economy. Service's once-reviled advice proved to be one of America's greatest strategic successes.

HUMILITY OVER HUBRIS

This may be Service's deepest lesson—and the one America most resists. Like me, Service was the child of missionaries. He understood the American impulse to "save" China and was certainly sympathetic to it. But Service tried to explain that China was not a blank slate for us to write our own script on. It had its own political dynamics and cultural traditions. America could influence these forces through engagement and example but never dictate them through pressure or wishful thinking.

Humility begins with the recognition that 1.4 billion people will chart their own course, like it or not.

Today's US–China relationship mirrors that of the late 1940s in unsettling ways. Once again, Washington confronts a China that refuses to fit American expectations. Once again, voices urging engagement are attacked as naïve or disloyal. And once again, the temptation is to mistake realism for weakness.

The echoes extend to domestic politics. Today, China hawks target business leaders, academics, and even former officials who advocate dialogue rather than confrontation. The accusations are strikingly similar: excessive sympathy for an authoritarian regime, insufficient patriotism, blindness to Chinese ambition, contamination by proximity.

I live in a similar middle space to Service. My work depends on fostering partnerships across the Pacific. In this climate of suspicion, I've felt the quiet doubts, the subtle insinuations about where my loyalties lie. No one has called me a traitor outright, but I fear that day is coming.

The John Service doctrine—see clearly, strip away ideology, accept reality, engage rather than isolate, approach others with humility—offers a path forward. It's not flashy. It won't go viral on social media. But it might prevent wars no one can win and isolation that serves no one's interests.

> **The John Service doctrine—see clearly, strip away ideology, accept reality, engage rather than isolate, approach others with humility—offers a path forward.**

John Service died in 1999, just as China was about to enter the WTO and step onto the global stage as a major economic power. He never lived to see China become America's primary strategic competitor. But his voice still whispers through the historical record, reminding us that true patriotism begins with the courage to see clearly and speak honestly, even when the truth is not what we want to hear.

BRING
JOBS
HOME
NO
MORE
CHINA
TRADE

PART II

OUR AMERICAN TRADE WITH CHINA, ON BALANCE

画蛇添足

(Huà shé tiān zú)

Adding legs to a perfectly good snake

BRING
JOBS
HOME
NO
MORE
CHINA
TRADE

CHAPTER 4

TRADE WAS FOR GOOD, REMEMBER?

When I was in college, free trade wasn't just theory—it was dogma. Adam Smith and Milton Friedman sat enthroned in every syllabus, their invisible hands gently guiding the global economy toward prosperity. But flash forward a couple decades, and suddenly, their disciples have gone rogue. Some of the same politicians who once genuflected at Davos now wave the banner of tariffs and trade wars like born-again mercantilists.

If Saint Adam of Kirkcaldy and Brother Milton of Chicago were to walk into a Washington trade hearing today—perhaps one discussing tariffs on Chinese semiconductors or restrictions on American AI exports—they'd look around in shock and disbelief. *Have you people lost your minds?*

And to be frank: Yes, we have.

If you haven't already guessed it, I am a fervent believer in free trade. Not because I converted in college but because I have seen the benefits of free trade with my own eyes and within the short span of my life.

I am a fervent believer in free trade. Not because I converted in college but because I have seen the benefits of free trade with my own eyes and within the short span of my life.

The Taiwan of my early childhood in the 1970s was still a predominantly agrarian society with a per capita GDP of around $350.[107] Japan was already at $2,000+ per capita GDP.[108] By the time I graduated from high school in 1988, Taiwan had urbanized, the economy had grown nearly twentyfold from the early 1970s, and the per capita GDP was over $6,000 (or $19,000 in today's dollars).[109] Fast-forward to today, and Taiwan is one of the wealthiest countries in the world, with the twenty-first largest economy; it is an absolute leader in semiconductors; and it has a per capita GDP of $33,437 as of 2024.[110]

Similarly, I spent most of my working career in China, where I saw the same thing happen there, with the country transforming from a mostly agrarian backwater in 1994 to the superpower it is today. As I work with new, non-China supply chains, I am watching this process play out in India, Indonesia, and Vietnam.

When economists said billions of people were being lifted out of poverty thanks to trade, I watched it happen. I lived it. I can still picture my neighbor in northern Taiwan, a quiet man with calloused hands, assembling bronze metal clips in his courtyard under a blue tarp roof: a makeshift factory in his own yard. Back then, his family cooked, studied, and slept all around this product waiting to be shipped to New York. Today, he lives in a high-rise condo with floor-to-ceiling windows where he receives his grandkids' FaceTime calls from Taiwan and the US. I've watched kids who grew up sleeping on straw mats become the first in their family to attend college, then watched their kids go on to study in California, Toronto, and Melbourne.

I remember the smells of the wet markets, the cries of street vendors, the rural alleys thick with bicycles and, occasionally, buffalo dung. I've watched those streets turn into six-lane arteries flanked by glass towers and glowing from nearby LED ads for phones and sneakers.

Trade didn't just change economies; it changed lives. It changed families. And once you've seen the transformation up close and personal, you can't unsee it.

Today, there are prominent politicians who throw cold water on the idea of free trade. Not because they doubt the benefits it brought to Taiwan, China, or Vietnam but because they believe those economies rose at the expense of ours—that their gain was America's loss.

Trade didn't just change economies; it changed lives. It changed families. And once you've seen the transformation up close and personal, you can't unsee it.

On one side, you have left-leaning labor critics, such as Bernie Sanders, who claim outsourcing through free trade allowed big corporations to send US jobs overseas, leading to the hollowing out of the middle class. On the other side, you have security hawks, such as Josh Hawley and Peter Navarro, who claim trade with China has emboldened and strengthened a civilizational adversary.

The most striking sentiment comes from Donald Trump, who said numerous times on the campaign trail, "We don't win on trade anymore."

Donald Trump is wrong. The United States wins massively on trade and has since the end of World War II.

While I will address labor concerns in depth in a later chapter, it is worth remembering why free trade became gospel in the first place and why America—rightly—was its most fervent disciple.

SPECIALIZING IN EFFICIENCY

In *The Wealth of Nations*, the foundational text of economics, Adam Smith developed a full-throated defense of free trade. Smith would have attacked the economic ideas the Trump administration has put forward in the first year of its second term with the ferocity of a Scottish Calvinist scorned. Smith despised the mercantilist notion that a nation grows richer by hoarding commodities and currency, maximizing exports, and minimizing imports. That mindset, he said, was economic superstition. Real wealth, he argued, came not from trade surpluses but from specialization, efficiency, and voluntary exchange. "It is the maxim of every prudent master of a family, never to attempt to make at home what it will cost him more to make than to buy."[111]

I've been personally involved in several industries in which manufacturing has returned to the US for political reasons, with projects made viable only through heavy subsidies or import restrictions. Take solar energy infrastructure, for example. Imagine a giant solar farm: row after row of panels mounted on long steel tubes, called torque tubes, that slowly turn to follow the sun. For years, they were made in China because Chinese mills could roll steel cheaply and at massive scale. Shipping them added freight costs, but even with various layers of countervailing tariffs, they were still the low-cost option up until 2021, when tariff barriers skyrocketed for imported steel and the US created new domestic incentives.

Under the Inflation Reduction Act, there's a big push to make torque tubes in the US. That sounds patriotic—and in some ways, it is—but there's a price. American-made tubes cost roughly \$0.40 to \$0.60 more per kilogram than the Chinese version. That doesn't sound like much until you realize that the infrastructure required to produce a megawatt of electricity uses twenty to thirty tons of steel just for the torque tubes. Multiply it out, and you're talking \$8,000–\$18,000 more per megawatt to pay for the torque tubes alone. To keep solar projects from grinding to a halt, the government now pays a subsidy of \$0.87 per kilogram of torque tube, which usually more than covers that extra cost. In other words, the solar field developer may think he's getting the same price, but we've just shifted who pays. Instead of the solar developer paying the higher price for US steel directly, US taxpayers are footing the bill through federal credits.

Of course, there may be legitimate political reasons for providing subsidies to certain industries. Having some domestic production of key infrastructure is smart insurance against trade wars, supply shocks, or national security risks. But it's important to be honest about what's happening: Reshoring doesn't happen on its own; buyers don't naturally gravitate to a more expensive price. It only happens with government support, where taxpayers are footing the bill.

Smith would not have liked subsidies at all, regardless of the political calculations.

Smith's most famous illustration of economic efficiency comes from his observation of a pin factory. There, he watched workers divide the production of pins into specialized tasks: One drew out the wire; another straightened it; another cut it, sharpened it, or attached the head. Eighteen separate operations in all. A single worker making pins alone might produce only one per day. But ten workers, each specializing in a single task, could produce forty-eight thousand pins a day. Divide the work, increase productivity, create wealth.

Smith saw this principle as applying to nations as well. A country should specialize in what it does best, trade for the rest, and let the market reward each accordingly. Smith's eighteenth-century trade example was Portuguese wine and English cloth: If Portugal could make better, cheaper wine and England better, cheaper cloth, both should specialize and trade. Simple and still true.

Or consider another industry example. Visit the pharmacy at any CVS or Walgreens to fill a prescription for a chronic condition. Odds are the diabetes, cholesterol, or blood pressure medication provided by your pharmacist was manufactured in India. But the billion-dollar patent? The decade of lab work, clinical trials, and FDA paperwork that brought it into being? That happened in Boston or San Diego.

This is Smith's pin factory on a planetary scale.

The US specializes in invention. It is home to six of the ten top pharmaceutical firms by research and development spend, with the others rounding out the list based in the EU.[112] In 2023, US pharmaceutical companies spent somewhere between $80 billion and $100 billion annually.[113]

Meanwhile, India specializes in production, manufacturing 47 percent of the generic drugs consumed in the US.[114] Once a drug goes off patent, Indian firms step in, producing high-quality medicine at a fraction of the cost. The US creates intellectual property and regulatory sophistication; India brings labor efficiency and mass production. Both sides win. And the world gets cheaper, safer medicine. It's an idea that works and has been shown to work in almost every industry, as long as it is allowed to work.

But all too often, the urge to protect home markets kicks in.

Protectionism, according to Smith, only wastes resources and props up inefficiencies. Worse, it forces the consumer to pay more—and for less.

Again, we can look at the pharma industry, where trade protectionism usually takes the form of attacking India's comparative advantage in manufacturing generics. Between 2013 and 2020, the US FDA significantly ramped up regulatory scrutiny of Indian pharmaceutical facilities. Plants were flagged with import bans or warning letters, often for lapses in documentation or quality control.[115] While some in the industry in India have accused US Big Pharma of lobbying for stricter oversight to curb competition, these claims remain unproven.

Still, the timing and scale of regulatory action led many in India to see it as a form of backdoor protectionism.

Regardless, the fallout was swift: Indian pharma's US revenue growth slowed, stock prices dipped, and global investors began to treat India's pharmaceutical export potential with caution. But what's less talked about is how this hurt American companies, hospitals, and consumers. Take the case of Ranbaxy Laboratories, once India's top generic medicine exporter. In 2013, the FDA banned imports from four of its plants. This came just as Ranbaxy was preparing to launch a generic version of NEXIUM (esomeprazole), a heartburn drug. With the Indian generic version delayed in the US market, AstraZeneca's patent-protected brand-name version kept raking in US sales of over $4 billion per year, and US consumers paid higher prices at pharmacies for far longer than necessary.[116] The lack of generic alternatives for this and hundreds of other medications cost US hospitals just as it cost ordinary consumers. Ironically, even US pharma giants suffered because many of them depend on Indian firms for low-cost active pharmaceutical ingredients—a dependency they have created to manage costs and scale production. When plants in India face bans or delays, these US firms are forced to find alternative sources, usually in Europe at much higher prices. Trying to wall off Indian generics may have protected short-term US pharma profits, but it sabotaged long-term efficiency and affordability and burdened American consumers with higher costs.

Global access to affordable medicine should be expanding, not shrinking, right? Isn't that what everyone is asking for? Unfettered free trade helps us get there.

When Adam Smith argued that protectionism only props up inefficiencies and when Milton Friedman warned that tariffs are just taxes with better PR, they were spot-on.

TRADE AS A LIBERTY

Two centuries after Smith, Milton Friedman picked up the torch and ran with it. Friedman's case for free trade was built not only on economic efficiency but also on personal liberty. He saw voluntary exchange as a form of freedom and government interference in trade as both economically harmful and ethically suspect: "The most important single central fact about a free market is that no exchange takes place unless both parties benefit."[117]

Friedman also believed that markets are information systems, with millions of buyers and sellers discovering costs, scarcities, and preferences through prices—what Friedrich Hayek famously called "the use of knowledge in society."

Nowhere is this clearer than in today's auto industry. A single EV sold in the US depends on thousands of parts sourced from dozens of countries: batteries from South Korea, advanced magnets from Australia, chips from Taiwan, safety glass from Canada, and final assembly in Tennessee or Michigan. Each component is purchased for a well-researched reason from the supplier most suited to making it, based on a combination of price and quality.

When we force automakers to buy from a domestic supplier only, we're limiting access to the highest-quality components at the best price. The policy feels patriotic, but the hidden price tag shows up in unexpected ways: higher sticker prices, EV rollouts that fall behind those of foreign competitors, and entire downstream industries—from charging networks to software startups—starved of the scale they need to grow.

Wasn't liberty, especially economic liberty, a foundational tenet of American life?

Wasn't there a tea party thingy about that?

SPECIALIZING EVEN WHEN YOU'RE SPECIAL

In 1827, David Ricardo, building on Adam Smith's insights, introduced the idea of comparative advantage: the principle that even if one country is more efficient at producing everything than another country, it should still specialize in what it does *relatively* better and trade for the rest. It's not about being the best at everything; it's about being better at what you're best at.

The best examples probably come from two companies from my childhood home of Taiwan: Foxconn (also known as Hon Hai Technology Group) and Taiwan Semiconductor Manufacturing Company (TSMC). Howard Lutnick, the US secretary of commerce, speaking on CBS's *Face the Nation* and failing to understand Ricardo's view about staying in your expertise lane, suggested that America needs to raise an "army of millions and millions of human beings screwing in little, little screws to make iPhones."[118] US expertise is in invention, remember? What we're not so good at is creating affordable labor. Are there millions and millions of Americans anxious to pass their days "screwing in little, little screws"? Would that be the best use of our vast educational and technological prowess? And is there, perhaps, a bit more to building an iPhone than screws?

TSMC, based in Hsinchu, Taiwan, manufactures over 90 percent of the globe's cutting-edge semiconductors, powering everything from iPhones to data centers to AI clusters. Foxconn, headquartered in New Taipei City, assembles the gadgets—iPhones, MacBooks, Xboxes, and Google Nest Hubs—with mind-bending efficiency. These Taiwanese companies have factories all over the world, with a special concentration in China. But what lands on American soil isn't just parts—it's the beginning of a massive value chain. TSMC's 3 nm chip, for instance, goes into Apple's latest processors. It allows the iPhone to run faster, cooler, and more securely. The same goes for Google, whose Pixel phones and AI servers rely on chips fabricated by TSMC. Or NVIDIA, which designs the world's most powerful GPUs and then has TSMC manufacture them before selling them into cloud clusters that power ChatGPT, DeepMind, and thousands of AI startups.

But the real value is what those chips unlock: Face ID, real-time rendering, 4K video editing, and AI processing. There is good money in the chips and gadgets that come from Taiwan. But the real money is in the trillion-dollar American software platforms, gaming engines, app stores, streaming empires, and AI breakthroughs that sit on top of them. TSMC doesn't design most of the chips it makes. Companies such as Apple, Google, NVIDIA, and AMD do. And all the products Foxconn assembles? It doesn't own the IP to any of them. That's the US's expertise. Not screws or the people manning little screwdrivers.

I don't call that exchange a deficit. We own the IP, and we remain the leader in creating the high-paying jobs that go with it. I call this a surplus of value in which the US is the overwhelming winner.

This is textbook comparative advantage.

The US is exceptional at high-end chip design, software integration, and building consumer ecosystems. Taiwan's TSMC is the undisputed master of precision chip fabrication, pouring tens of billions into fabrication labs. And after decades of experience, Foxconn can marshal the labor output of hundreds of thousands of people and reach enormous scale on a new model in just weeks. Each party focuses on what it does best. Each wins by not trying to do it all.

This is exactly what Ricardo meant. Even if one country could design *and* build such products, it gains more by doing what it's relatively better at and trading for the rest. The US could build all the fabrication plants it needs to make every advanced chip at home; it could have an army of people putting in those tiny iPhone screws.

But why would we? That would take decades, cost trillions, and burn immense political capital. Meanwhile, Apple, Google, and NVIDIA would be dragged into the silicon trenches of chip and gadget production, trying to replicate what TSMC and Foxconn already do instead of racing ahead in design and maximizing the customer experience.

Let's look at just a couple of other vastly different sectors in which we see similar, very real American competitive advantage at risk. Consider agriculture. American farms don't just feed America; they feed the world. In 2024, US agricultural exports hit $176 billion thanks to a mix of North American Free Trade Agreement (NAFTA) legacy deals, WTO access, and insatiable demand from China, Japan, and beyond. Corn, soybeans, beef, dairy—these are global staples, and we are the global supplier.[119] Why? Because we have the space, because of scale, because of precision farming and genetically modified crops, and because of a logistical supply chain no other country can match. We dominate this space.

And yet, when tariff wars flare up, guess who's always the first target for Chinese retaliation? Iowa farmers. Kansas cattlemen. The guys doing everything right. And in 2025, in the age of new tariffs, guess which world leader in soybean consumption stopped buying American soybeans.

Then there's higher education, which isn't just a cultural export—it's a real economic one. In 2023, international students brought over $38 billion into the US economy.[120] These students pay full tuition, rent apartments, eat takeout, buy cars, and often go on to found startups, work for Fortune 500 companies, or become doctors in Midwestern towns that badly need them. I've worked with many of these people. When we slap tariffs or visa restrictions on certain countries in the name of national security, we start to look paranoid, not prudent. And we undercut one of our most quietly profitable exports: knowledge.

Are we really going to divert corporate and national resources away from the trillions of dollars of revenue we currently realize so that we can get in on the mere hundreds of billions of revenue we don't realize but control anyway?

I hope not.

FREE TRADE MADE IN THE USA

If protectionism imagines a strong America behind a wall, the real economy tells a different story: one not just about comparative advantage but of the collaboration and free trade that fuel US dominance.

Point to any big-box shelf and you'll see "Made in China" everywhere. The easy conclusion is this: America buys, China wins. But the real story misses the hundreds of thousands of US small- and medium-sized enterprises (SMEs) wedged between the US big-box retailer and the Chinese factory: the designers, inventors, brand owners, compliance teams, warehouses, and marketers capturing fat chunks of margin at home. The factory in Suzhou may make the retractable garden hose, but an American team in Tennessee had the idea, created the brand and the sales channel, and holds a lot of value that the trade hawks in Washington seem to miss.

If we're looking at the roughly $1.5 trillion in combined revenue between Costco, Walmart, and Amazon, how is all that money split up? In 2023, Costco, Walmart, and Amazon made $50 billion in combined net profit. Those numbers are easy to find; they're publicly listed companies. The profit across the American SMEs is harder to find, as they are mostly private companies. But based on a general knowledge of their profit margins, it is likely they collectively pulled in north of $100 billion in net profit. And what about the Chinese manufacturers who make the stuff? They get a cut, of course, but it's not nearly as large as people assume. According to China's National Bureau of Statistics, industrial manufacturers typically operate on profit margins around 4–5 percent. World Bank and OECD value-chain studies show Chinese OEM factories often capture just 3–10 percent of the final retail price. In real terms, on a $100 gadget sold at Costco, the factory in Dongguan might keep only $3–$6 in profit.[121]

For all the bluster about how China's "winning" at trade, the math seems to suggest that US companies are capturing as much as 75 percent of the value chain and the Chinese manufacturer maybe 25 percent.

I don't see that we're losing in trade.

But if you want to see how we do end up losing, let me tell you about my sister.

She runs one of those SMEs, a company called Bunnies By The Bay. It is one of the cutest yet toughest companies I have ever known. On the surface, it's a company that designs and sells plush bunny rabbits, animal dolls, and books for babies.

But, really, it is a sisterhood.

This sisterhood started in 1983 with a fishing boat disaster, when three male members of a family were lost because a crabbing boat capsized in stormy Alaskan seas, leaving a clutch of women in Anacortes, Washington, widowed or fatherless. These women started gathering for coffee and cake and drew comfort from doing needlework together, a tradition passed down from their Nordic grandmothers.

Two sisters among these women, Krys and Suzanne, were especially creative and soon found they could make a small living creating designer collectible bunny rabbits. These rabbits were adorable but sold for hundreds of dollars (think bunnies in Victorian dresses).

My sister—who, like me, grew up in Taiwan and did business in China—met Krys and Suzanne when Bunnies was still a young, struggling business. At the time, it was one of only two companies manufacturing plush toys in the US—the other being the Vermont Teddy Bear company. But the business was not sustainable. My sister fell in love with Bunnies By The Bay and advised Krys and Suzanne, "Hey, we need to diversify; to make this business work, you need some bunnies that can retail for $20 sitting alongside the collectible ones selling for $200, and in the US, that's impossible to pull off. I know a bunch of Taiwanese-owned family-run factories in China who can help you." They joined forces and built a great little business.

Bunnies By The Bay has thirty-nine employees in Anacortes, and it has a design and product development team, a sales team, a warehouse that does online fulfillment, and a finance team led by my niece. The company now makes gifts, baby security blankets, plush toys, and a library of children's books. The commercial and creative action is 100 percent housed in Washington state.

But yes, there is one factory in China making most of the Bunnies products.

Contrary to the media narrative, that China factory has become part of the Bunnies family. The factory works on tiny margins, puts in long weeks, and has gone out of its way to make life easy for Bunnies—including agreeing to not being paid for extended periods, as American banks offer meager support for small businesses such as Bunnies.

It's a partnership that works. One side manufactures the product; the other side does the creative design, the marketing, and the sales. Bunnies is in FAO Schwarz, Hallmark, and Barnes &

Noble, and it supplies countless mom-and-pop gift stores and has a vibrant online presence.

Recently, after many years of trying, Bunnies finally negotiated an order with Costco—the kind of order that opens huge markets. The order was to start shipping on May 9, 2025, but suddenly, one month before the products were to ship, the Trump administration placed a 145 percent tariff on them. Costco called and said, "Don't ship."

Bunnies had stretched big for that order, borrowing money from family and friends, and if the order were to be cancelled, Bunnies By The Bay would be sailing into dangerous financial waters.

The tariff was eventually lowered to a combined rate of 30 percent. Costco called and allowed shipping to resume. But at that tariff rate, the sticker price increased from $16.95 to $25.95 for a plush Easter bunny, and even with that increase, neither Costco nor Bunnies made much money on the order. The two companies moved the product just to keep the gears turning.

Here's the greatest irony: The Chinese factory never had to change its price. The tariff greatly reduced the 75 percent profit margin that belonged to the US but preserved in whole the 25 percent that goes to China.

Is it just me, or is that really stupid?!

There was no scenario in which Bunnies could quickly have had these goods made in the US. Toys like this have been made out of the country for many decades, preceding the rise of China. And there is no one—I mean not one worker, investor, or manufacturing group—who is lining up to take on this kind of work. There is simply—obviously—not enough money in it.

On paper, and to people who don't know how to read them, trade numbers look like a tidal wave of Chinese dominance. But take a closer look at where many of these goods start, and it's with SMEs like Bunnies By The Bay. From cookware brands in Ohio to bike part designers in Colorado to baby monitor startups in California, most of what's manufactured in China is actually imagined, prototyped, funded, and marketed in the United States. The factories might reside in Dongguan or Suzhou, but the ideas, the branding, and the logistics are American made. And like Apple, it is the US entities that are reaping most of the benefit.

Ladies and gentlemen, we were winning at trade; we had been for a long time. Why are we trying to shut it down?

Ladies and gentlemen, we were winning at trade; we had been for a long time. Why are we trying to shut it down?

THE NUMBERS DON'T LIE: AMERICA'S HIDDEN TRADE ADVANTAGES

All the talk of trade deficits misses something else entirely: America's massive services surplus. In 2024, the US ran a services surplus of $293.3 billion—financial services, software licensing, intellectual property, higher education, entertainment.[122] The deficit numbers everyone obsesses over only count the physical goods, not the trillion-dollar ecosystems of American value creation.

Consider job creation. A 2021 Business Roundtable study found that international trade supported over forty-one million American jobs—that's one in five US jobs. Of these, more than twenty-eight million provided middle-class incomes, and over fifteen million were held by minority workers.[123] Meanwhile, exports alone supported 10.2 million jobs in 2022, with each billion dollars of exports supporting approximately 4,100 jobs.[124]

Trade-dependent employment has grown four times faster than overall US employment since 1992. These aren't just any jobs; they're concentrated in America's most competitive sectors: aerospace, technology, agriculture, financial services, and intellectual property–

intensive industries that command premium wages. Imports support American jobs. These are the workers in logistics, retail, quality control, marketing, and distribution who make global supply chains function on American soil. The China trade is only partially about China; it is just as much about truckers in Ohio, software engineers in Seattle, and marketing teams in Manhattan.

LESSONS FROM HISTORY: WHEN PROTECTIONISM GOES WRONG

Before we completely abandon the free trade consensus that built American prosperity, perhaps we should remember what happened the last time we decided to protect American industry from foreign competition.

In June 1930, President Herbert Hoover signed the Smoot-Hawley Tariff Act into law, raising tariffs on over twenty thousand imported goods by an average of 20 percent.[125] More than one thousand economists had signed a petition urging Hoover to veto the legislation. Even Henry Ford spent an evening at the White House trying to convince the president to reject what he called "an economic stupidity."[126]

Hoover signed it anyway.

The results were catastrophic. Twenty-three trading partners immediately protested, and twenty-four countries imposed retaliatory tariffs within two years. Canada, America's largest trading partner, imposed new duties on American goods and turned toward closer economic ties with the British Empire. Global trade collapsed by 66 percent between 1929 and 1934. US exports to Europe fell from $2.3 billion to $784 million. US imports from Europe dropped from $1.3 billion to just $390 million.[127]

The tariffs didn't save American jobs—they destroyed them. Unemployment jumped from 8 percent at the time Smoot-Hawley was passed to 16 percent in 1931 and 25 percent by 1933.[128] Export-dependent industries were devastated. Farmers, whom the tariffs were originally supposed to protect, saw their exports fall by one-third.

Most economists now agree that Smoot-Hawley didn't cause the Great Depression, but it significantly deepened and prolonged it. The tariffs created a beggar-thy-neighbor dynamic that made the global economic crisis worse for everyone, including America. The lesson was so clear that Smoot-Hawley became a watchword for the dangers of protectionism. Beginning with the Reciprocal Trade Agreements Act of 1934, the United States spent the next eighty years leading the world toward freer trade. That leadership helped create the prosperity we enjoy today.

Ronald Reagan, hardly a liberal internationalist, understood this history. "The Smoot-Hawley tariff ignited an international trade war and helped sink our country into the Great Depression," he said in a radio address in 1986.[129]

Are we really sure we want to repeat that experiment?

Today's tariffs may be aimed at Beijing, but they spray shrapnel at home. Our brands, our workers, our consumers are collateral damage. Smith, Ricardo, and Friedman already warned us.

We should continue to listen.

CHAPTER 5

CONTAGIONS ENTERING OUR OPEN DOOR

Two hundred years of American history—and a mountain of data—show that free trade has been a blessing for this country. As economist Douglas Irwin puts it, "There is arguably no proposition more widely held among economists than the free trade of goods across countries generally benefits the citizens of both the exporting and the importing countries."[130] Trade is not a zero-sum game. It has lifted more boats than it has swamped. On balance, far more people have benefited from it than have not.

I am unapologetic about this. I'm not alone. Survey after survey finds that roughly nine out of ten economists agree that free trade increases overall welfare.[131] You don't need a PhD to see why. Free trade has given us cheaper goods, growing markets for American innovators, and a way to connect with the world without sending soldiers.

Free trade is good. Period.

But it would be naïve—and, frankly, foolish—to pretend free trade hasn't carried costs. Yes, since the late 1980s, some American towns were hollowed out. Trust was frayed as ideas crossed borders without clear rules. And the planet groaned under the weight of our global industrial surge.

If free trade is an open door, we keep it open because it brings in sunlight, fresh air, and new possibilities. But it also lets in dust, drafts, and the occasional mosquito carrying an unknown contagion. Our task is not to slam the door shut and seal ourselves inside; that leads to stagnation and horribly stale air. Nor is it to fling the door wide open without a thought for what might enter. The challenge is to manage the opening wisely—install the right screens, so to speak.

Let's examine these contagions. Some are real threats, though often misunderstood; others are yesterday's problems, already fading; and some are simply chronic conditions to be managed, not cured.

THE TRADE DEFICIT: A HEMORRHAGE OR NOT?

In 2005, Senator Chuck Schumer described America's growing trade deficit as "a slow bleeding at the wrists economically for the United States."[132] It's a vivid image, one that has stuck in the public imagination. Trade deficits are often portrayed as a hemorrhage: money flowing out, strength draining away, America weakening by the day.

And the numbers can look alarming. According to the US Bureau of Economic Analysis, recent US goods-trade deficits have reached historic highs—approaching the trillion-dollar mark in recent years.[133] Most of that gap came from imports of manufactured goods from countries such as China, Mexico, Germany, and Vietnam, while our biggest export categories—aircraft, agricultural products, and high-end industrial machinery—couldn't keep pace. On a purely surface read, it looks like we're shipping dollars abroad and getting only "stuff" in return.

But is that really what a trade deficit means? Not really. As we've seen, fabled economists Smith, Ricardo, and Friedman didn't see trade deficits as national wounds. They saw it as one side of a two-sided coin. They are joined by modern free trade champions such as Paul Krugman, Douglas Irwin, and Jagdish Bhagwati.

A trade deficit means foreigners are sending goods to us, yes, but they are also investing their surplus dollars back into our economy, buying stocks, bonds, real estate, or US Treasury bills. This return flow of dollars—what economists call the round trip—is how international finance naturally balances. When the US buys a $40,000 car made in South Korea, those dollars don't remain idle in Seoul. They flow back into the US, often to finance the very loans Americans use to buy homes, start businesses, or send kids to college.

Historically, this cycle has had some powerful benefits. In the 1980s and 1990s, foreign capital inflows helped keep US interest rates lower, fueling an unprecedented wave of innovation and startup growth. Even today, foreign investors hold about $8 trillion in US Treasury securities, effectively subsidizing our government borrowing at cheaper rates than it could otherwise afford.[134] The trade deficit, in other words, comes with a built-in return ticket for dollars. As Paul Krugman once put it, trade deficits are often a sign that foreign investors think your economy is a good bet.[135] It's a far less dramatic image than Schumer's bleeding wrists, but far closer to the truth.

MR. LIN'S DEFICIT THAT WASN'T AND MS. CHEN'S LOCKED CAPITAL

I understand this because of Mr. Lin. He is a family friend who owns a shoe factory in Taichung, Taiwan. For three decades, his family business produced athletic footwear for American brands. In the early years, his shoes went to discount retailers. As the quality and scale of his factory improved, he began supplying bigger names, household brands you'd find in every US mall. On paper, you'd see a one-way street: Taiwan exporting, America importing. From a protectionist's perspective, Mr. Lin was part of the deficit "problem."

But Mr. Lin didn't stash his US earnings in offshore accounts. In the early 2000s, he applied for the EB-5 Program and invested in a cluster of 7Eleven franchises in Southern California. The EB-5 Immigrant Investor Program allows foreign nationals to obtain a US green card by making a qualifying investment in a US business that creates or preserves at least ten full-time jobs for US workers. Mr. Lin paid US taxes, hired American workers, and later funded his children's education at Purdue University, Michigan, and UCLA—paying full international tuition. Given the opportunity, he invested in the US economy.

Revisit the ledger with that in mind. What looks like a loss in the trade accounts was, in reality, a circle of shared prosperity, denominated in dollars.

But Mr. Lin's example isn't to say the trade deficit isn't a problem. In the case of China, it is a unique problem. With other governments, when the US runs a trade deficit, the dollars we send abroad eventually return when foreigners buy American goods, services, or financial assets. As Michael Pettis explains, "If China ran its surplus the way other countries do, the dollars it earns would come back to the US as spending or investment. But China's system of capital controls prevents that, so the money piles up as foreign exchange reserves instead."[136]

What makes China's trade surplus uniquely problematic isn't its size alone—Germany actually runs a larger trade surplus as a percentage of GDP.[137] The difference is that Germans can freely invest their savings in American stocks, bonds, or real estate. Chinese savers cannot. This blocked circulation creates what Pettis calls "forced saving" in China and "forced borrowing" in deficit countries such as the US. China deliberately blocks the return flow, hoarding US dollars. This distorts the normal mechanics of trade, creating what Pettis calls an "unbalanced balance."[138] It's like a poker game where one player never spends their winnings but just keeps stacking chips, warping the game for everyone else. America gets the goods but not the reciprocal benefits of foreign investment and demand that should follow. Over time, that leaves the US economy bearing more of the adjustment costs, while China gains an artificial boost to its export sector and domestic savings rate.

If Mr. Lin showed me how open finance can balance trade, Ms. Chen showed me what happens when it can't. Ms. Chen is single and works for a European multinational in Shanghai. She's smart, sharp with numbers, and saves about a third of her income, like many middle-class professionals in China. But she can't freely invest those savings abroad. China's capital account is so tightly controlled that, in 2023, individuals were limited to just $50,000 per year in foreign transfers—a cap unchanged for over a decade.[139] Even reaching that limit requires layers of paperwork and approvals. She would love to buy a small flat in Vancouver, invest in a US index fund, or put money into her cousin's startup in Singapore. Instead, her savings are trapped in a state-run bank, earning minimal interest. The bank recycles her deposits into low-interest loans for state-linked industries—steel, glass, electronics—which in turn produce more exports.

In other words, Ms. Chen's trapped savings become part of the very machine that sustains China's trade surplus. If their capital could move, people like Ms. Chen could help ease the imbalance.

While we should acknowledge that our trade deficit with China is an issue, tariffs are the wrong instrument to use to address it. They make imports more expensive for American consumers and downstream industries, and they do nothing to free up China's locked capital or empower Chinese households. At worst, they strengthen Beijing's hand by tightening state control.

Rather than caring about how many shoes Mr. Lin exports, we should fight for Ms. Chen's right to choose where her savings go. Only when that happens can the free trade ledger reflect real reciprocity.

INTELLECTUAL PROPERTY, STATE SUBSIDIES, AND THE GRAY ZONE OF TRUST

If trade deficits are an accounting issue, intellectual property is a trust issue. Few topics have caused more bitterness in US–China relations. For decades, American companies and policymakers have accused China of copying designs, pirating software, hacking servers, and forcing technology transfers as the price of market access. These concerns are not theoretical. According to a 2019 US Trade Representative report, the estimated annual cost to the US economy from Chinese IP theft ranged from $225 billion to $600 billion—roughly equivalent to the entire US agricultural sector. In sectors such as aerospace, pharmaceuticals, and high-tech manufacturing, these losses are seen not merely as commercial setbacks but as threats to national competitiveness.

The result has been an atmosphere of deep suspicion. US firms remember high-profile cases such as the theft of DuPont's Kevlar fiber technology or the Department of Justice's 2014 indictment of five Chinese military hackers accused of stealing data from US steel and energy companies.[140] These stories fed a powerful narrative: China doesn't innovate; it copies. It doesn't play by the rules.

But reality—as usual—is messier.

EVERYDAY IP THEFT: THE VIEW FROM THE FACTORY FLOOR

Let's start with the kind of IP infringement I know best: plain old everyday IP theft. These are the stories that play out in the trenches of regular company-to-company relationships. These are the stories I've lived over and over again. And here, most cases begin not with criminal conspiracy but with a fragile handshake.

Don't get me wrong—some complaints from US companies have been absolutely justified. I've seen cases of outright theft: molds disappearing overnight, proprietary designs reappearing at a competitor's booth at a trade fair, patents ignored with impunity. There's no excuse for it. But that kind of theft happens far less than people imagine.

Far more often, the stories are less about criminal intent and more about misaligned incentives and shallow relationships. American buyers, under relentless pressure to deliver quarterly cost reductions, would squeeze their Chinese suppliers until there was no fat left to trim. A supplier who had invested heavily in new machinery, trained workers, and built custom tooling to meet a US customer's needs might suddenly find that same customer walking away to save two cents a unit with a competitor down the street.

Especially in the early days, foreign buyers tended to think of Chinese suppliers as disposable tools—easily discarded, easily replaced. That mentality had its result: an equal and opposite counterreaction.

This is the gray zone between collaboration and competition, and it is wide. It's a space in which relationships matter more than legal documents. American executives sometimes forget that contracts are not magical shields. In China—as in much of the world—the real enforcement mechanism is the strength of the relationship. When that relationship is strong, both sides win and are yoked around achieving the same goal. In those cases, IP is generally safe.

The fact that the volume of the US–China trade relationship has grown to such an extent illustrates that the vast majority of our commercial relationships are healthy, with mutual trust well in place. But when that trust frays, when a trading relationship can be tossed aside while chasing pennies, it gets complicated. If you have a manufacturer who knows your product as well as you do, who knows how to improve on it, and who then feels they are not respected as a partner, the temptation to repurpose designs or shift production quietly grows stronger.

MR. JIANG'S QUANDARY

Mr. Jiang's story may be helpful here. (And for the record, I know scores of Mr. Jiangs.) He was a factory owner in southern China making basic electronics for mostly American buyers: wine fridges, LED lighting, and pumps that blow up inflatable beds, among others. He built his business investing in equipment, training skilled workers, and delivering to the exacting specifications of his American customers. For years, his livelihood depended on those orders.

Then, abruptly, his major buyer pulled its orders. Not because Mr. Jiang failed to deliver but because another factory offered the same products for a little less. Everyone goes to China for the cheap price, after all, and so when you find that cheaper price, it's hard not to take it. There was no handshake, no thank-you, no transition plan. Just a terse email: "We've decided to move in another direction."

Mr. Jiang was left with idle machines he'd purchased to meet US demand, workers he could no longer pay, and a warehouse full of inventory. Facing likely ruin, he repurposed his product, added Chinese labels, and altered the tooling so he could sell in China's domestic market.

From a US perspective, his shift of the product to the Chinese market was IP theft, since the product had been built to specs given by the US customer. Mr. Jiang was later served with cease and desist papers from an international law firm with an office in Shanghai. But from Mr. Jiang's perspective, changing his customer base was survival. The US company had abandoned him, he reasoned. They only sold this product in America, so why would they care if he sold a version in China? "Why should I just shut down," he asked me, "when they abandoned me first?"

Yet, the dynamic has begun to change. As Chinese firms climb the value chain and start selling their own products, they now need IP protection of their own. Beijing has responded with specialized IP courts, tougher enforcement, and more consistent judgments, including cases in which foreign firms prevail.[141] Such changes aren't about Chinese firms adopting Western norms because they've been lectured to; they are about self-preservation. China has become a leading inventor, not just a manufacturer.

STATE-SPONSORED SUPPORT: WHEN NATIONS COMPETE

When we zoom out from factory floors to state strategy, the story shifts from gray to geopolitical. This is not my area of expertise, but I follow developments with great interest. The rise of Huawei and BYD—two great symbols of China's technological ascent—illustrates how industrial ambition, state subsidy, and intellectual property collide on the world stage. These are not simply corporate success stories. They are monuments to a particular vision of how nations compete in the twenty-first century.

HUAWEI: FROM IMITATION TO INNOVATION

In *House of Huawei: The Secret History of China's Most Powerful Company*, journalist Eva Dou traces Huawei's transformation from a small Shenzhen startup in 1987 to a global telecom giant controlling nearly a third of the world's telecommunications infrastructure by 2020.[142] She describes its early years as a mix of improvisation and imitation, noting that the company copied Western equipment design in ways that would be impossible in a mature IP regime.[143]

The details are revealing. In the 1990s, Huawei reverse engineered switches from Nortel and Cisco, studying their architecture with forensic precision. Former employees have testified to a corporate culture that treated Western patents as suggestions rather than boundaries. In the early 2000s, Cisco sued Huawei for copying its router software—including identical bugs in the code. The case settled quietly, with Huawei agreeing to modify its products, but the damage to its reputation lingered.

Yet this is only half the story. By 2010, Huawei had become one of the world's largest filers of international patents. It poured 10 to 15 percent of revenue into R&D annually—a rate that rivaled or exceeded Western peers.[144] The company that once imitated had become, in many domains, the innovator. Its 5G technology, by most technical assessments, led the world.

Huawei also became the embodiment of China's technological nationalism: A champion too big to fail.[145] The Chinese government provided cheap credit through state banks, procurement preferences through telecom ministries, and diplomatic support through its embassies worldwide. When the US blacklisted Huawei in 2019, Beijing responded with fury, framing the ban as an attempt to suppress Chinese innovation and preserve American hegemony.

BYD: THE ELECTRIC COLOSSUS

BYD's trajectory mirrors Huawei's in instructive ways. Founded in 1995 as a battery manufacturer in Shenzhen, BYD entered the automotive industry in 2003 by acquiring a failing state-owned car company. For years, it produced cheap, unremarkable vehicles for the domestic market. Then came the pivot.

Under China's New Energy Vehicle mandate, launched in 2009 and turbocharged under Made in China 2025, BYD received a cascade of support: subsidies for EV purchases (up to $10,000 per vehicle), preferential access to license plates in congested cities, low-interest loans from China Development Bank, and protection from foreign competition through joint venture requirements.[146] Local governments competed to host BYD factories, offering land at below-market rates and tax holidays stretching years into the future.

The subsidy structure was labyrinthine by design. Provincial governments offered rebates that technically fell outside WTO restrictions on central state aid. Export financing came through policy banks rather than direct treasury outlays. The result was a system that appeared decentralized but functioned with coordinated purpose.

By 2023, BYD had surpassed Tesla to become the world's largest seller of EVs. Its Blade Battery technology—safer and more energy dense than that of competitors—represented genuine innovation.[147] But Western rivals argued that the company never would have reached scale without subsidies that totaled, by some estimates, tens of billions of dollars over two decades.[148]

THREE TRUTHS IN TENSION

To make sense of this landscape, three observations seem unavoidable, even if they sit uneasily together.

First, China has mastered the art of exploiting legal gray zones. Regional grants, export rebates, soft loans, and tax holidays allow Beijing to accelerate key sectors while remaining, at least nominally, within WTO parameters. These subsidies are often provincial rather than central, making them harder to classify as prohibited state aid under international trade law. When challenged, Chinese officials point to agricultural supports in Europe or defense subsidies in America, arguing that every major power plays this game—China simply plays it with greater focus.[149]

Second, Western firms have been willing participants in technology transfer. Apple built its entire supply chain in China, training thousands of engineers in precision manufacturing. (You can read more on that in *Apple in China: The Capture of the World's Greatest Company.*)[150] Tesla opened a gigafactory in Shanghai and shared battery technology with Chinese partners. Boeing established a completion center in Zhoushan that brought advanced aerospace knowledge to Chinese soil.[151] Much of what looks like theft in the rearview mirror was, at the time, a negotiated exchange: market access and lower costs in return for technical knowledge. Western executives made these deals clear-eyed, even if policymakers now regret the cumulative effect.

Third—and perhaps most importantly—China feels historically entitled to catch up. Over dinner one night in Hangzhou, a mid-level commerce official, Mr. Wang, put it bluntly: "Why do the Americans have to own everything? Our whole history is the West lording their tech over us, controlling us with it. The Opium Wars, the Eight-Nation Alliance, a century of humiliation. Now we finally have our own technology to protect ourselves, and you call it theft?"

That sense of moral debt runs deep. To Mr. Wang, and to many in Beijing, technology control is a kind of emancipation, not aggression. It's the restoration of what was taken, the reclamation of dignity. As I've mentioned, this narrative—cultivated in schools, celebrated in state media, internalized by a generation of engineers and policymakers—shapes how China approaches industrial policy. It says subsidies are not distortions; they're good governance. It says IP questions are exaggerated, and that China deserves to have its own domain of tech influence.

Whether this framing justifies the means is a question that divides not just nations but also trade lawyers, ethicists, and economists. What is harder to dispute is that China's approach has worked. Huawei and BYD show that state-directed capitalism, when executed with patience and capital, can compete with—and in some domains surpass—the innovations of the market-led West.

At least in the short term ...

Whether the country will ever make a return on its trillion dollars in industry support is also subject to debate.

BUILDING TRUST AT SCALE

The question now is what comes next.

I've argued that low-level IP theft is best prevented through solid relationships—through treating suppliers as partners, investing in mutual success, and creating incentives for long-term collaboration.

The same principle applies at the national level, though the scale is far greater and the stakes far higher. Just as Mr. Jiang needed respect and predictability from his American buyer, China needs space to pursue its national ambitions without feeling that every step toward technological advancement will be met with accusations of cheating or threats of containment. And just as American companies need assurance that their investments won't be copied and their IP won't be used against them, the United States needs confidence that China's rise doesn't come at the expense of a rules-based global order.

Both goals are possible.

This doesn't mean accepting unfair practices or ignoring genuine theft. It means recognizing that confrontation alone breeds the very distrust that makes IP violations more likely. When nations feel cornered, when they believe the existing system is rigged against them, they have little incentive to play by rules they perceive as illegitimate.

What's needed is a framework that allows both sides to achieve their core goals while establishing clear, boring, predictable platforms on which contentious issues can be addressed before they explode into crises. The US–China Strategic and Economic Dialogue, which operated from 2009 to 2017, was one such mechanism—flawed and frustrating, but a place where grievances could be aired and deals could be struck.[152] Its suspension marked a turn toward mutual hostility that has served neither side well.

We need new versions of that dialogue. Forums in which American concerns about subsidies, forced technology transfer, and cyber theft can be raised consistently and China can articulate its development needs without being dismissed as a revisionist power.

Mr. Jiang and his American buyer never rebuilt their relationship. The legal threats hardened into resentment, and Mr. Jiang's dominant supply to the China market has ensured his former US customer has no chance of ever getting in.

It didn't have to end that way.

ENVIRONMENTAL COSTS: SMOKE IN THE GLOBAL COMMONS

In the United States, policymakers had spent decades tightening environmental rules to ensure cleaner production. When those industries went offshore, America's skies cleared, but China's darkened. As many rightly claim, we outsourced our pollution.

From the late 1990s through the 2010s, China became known as the world's factory. Its share of global manufacturing output soared from just 7 percent in 1990 to over 30 percent by 2022, according to the United Nations Industrial Development Organization.[153] That explosive growth came with an equally explosive rise in emissions. By 2006, China had surpassed the United States to become the world's largest emitter of CO_2.[154] Today, China accounts for roughly 30 percent of global carbon emissions, more than the US and EU combined.[155]

In 2013, Beijing experienced the infamous Airpocalypse, when particulate matter (PM2.5) levels reached nearly forty times the World Health Organization's safe limit.[156] A 2015 study published in *Nature* estimated that air pollution contributed to 1.6 million premature deaths annually in China, roughly 4,000 deaths per day.[157] Rivers told a similar story. By 2011, Chinese environmental-science research and media reporting revealed that vast numbers of China's rivers suffered pollution levels so severe that whole basins—especially in industrial or mining regions—were effectively unusable for drinking or bathing.[158]

But Beijing wasn't blind to the smog or the poisoned waterways. It made a deliberate choice: Advance first, fix later. This wasn't unique to China. Every country that has industrialized has gone through a similarly dirty phase. Britain's Industrial Revolution left London coated in coal soot. In the United States, the Cuyahoga River caught fire multiple times, with the most famous blaze in 1969 helping to spark the creation of the Environmental Protection Agency.

China's leaders followed the same line knowingly, betting that a rich nation could clean up faster and more effectively than a poor one. Between 2013 and 2017, after launching its aggressive war on pollution, China reduced average urban PM2.5 levels by 35 percent, according to research by the University of Chicago.[159] That's an environmental turnaround at a speed and scale unmatched in history.

No one expressed this economically rich/environmentally poor tradeoff more plainly than Mr. Wei, a county official in Anhui province, central China, whose local economy revolved around hotdip galvanizing—a process of coating steel with zinc to prevent corrosion. The process is basic but messy: chemical baths, molten zinc, acrid fumes, and the ever present risk of waste finding its way into waterways.

Over tea around 2010, Mr. Wei gestured toward the huge outdoor zinc baths. "We know this isn't perfect," he said. "But for now, this is what we can afford." For generations, the county had been poor: subsistence farming, outmigration, dilapidated roads, polluted rivers. The galvanizing plants, which were kicked out of urban areas such as Shanghai or Chongqing, were finding their way to rural Anhui. And that changed everything: more jobs at home, tax revenue for schools and clinics, and a budding local services economy.

Mr. Wei likened the county to a rocket: Pollution was the smoke of launch. The goal wasn't to fly dirty forever but to escape the gravity of poverty, then clean up. "We can live with this in the short term," he said, "so that in ten years, we can build beautiful parks and clear water projects."

I returned to Anhui a decade later. Incomes had grown, a new hospital had opened, roads were paved, and plans for a riverside park were underway, funded by the very factories that dirtied the riverbanks.

THE TURNING POINT: CITIZENS PUSH BACK

Like in Anhui, in the early 2010s, the smog became unbearable all over China. Middle-class families acted: checking AQI apps before school, sharing photos of blackened skies, pressing officials quietly but persistently. A watershed moment arrived with Chai Jing's viral documentary *Under the Dome*, which racked up hundreds of millions of views before censors pulled it.[160] The message was unmistakable: We endured the smoke to build this country; now we want clean air for our children.

Out of necessity, Beijing listened. Smog had become a political threat to stability. Coal use plateaued; investment surged into solar, wind, nuclear, and EVs; and air quality in cities such as Beijing improved markedly. There have been complications, of course, but the environmental difference today is substantial, and awareness has entered much of the national psyche.

There's irony too. Those grimy, coal-powered factories that once filled the skies with soot also built the hardware of the global green transition: solar panels, wind turbines, lithium-ion batteries, and EVs. In the process, China has gone from environmental villain to the world's dominant supplier of clean energy technologies.

The scale of this transformation is staggering.

- **Solar power:** In 2005, China produced less than 10 percent of the world's solar panels. By 2023, it produced over 80 percent of global solar photovoltaic modules.[161] Of the world's ten largest solar manufacturers, eight are Chinese. China also accounts for 97 percent of global production of solar wafers, the core component of every solar panel.[162]
- **Wind energy:** China now leads the world in wind turbine production and installation. In 2023 alone, it installed over sixty-nine gigawatts of new wind power capacity—more than the rest of the world combined.[163]
- **Lithium batteries:** China dominates the global EV battery supply chain. It produces over 75 percent of the world's lithium-ion batteries and controls 70 percent of cathode production and 85 percent of anode production.[164] This has positioned Chinese companies such as CATL and BYD as indispensable suppliers, not just for Chinese EV makers but also for Tesla, BMW, and other Western brands.

- **Electric vehicles:** In 2023, China became the world's largest exporter of cars, largely because of its EV boom. BYD alone sold 3.02 million EVs, surpassing Tesla's 1.8 million.[165]

This green boom goes into domestic consumption, but it's also an export machine. China accounts for "three-quarters of global investments" in clean technologies such as solar PV, batteries, and other elements of clean energy technology.[166] For every solar farm built in Texas or Bavaria, chances are the panels were manufactured in Jiangsu or Sichuan. In 2023, non–fossil fuel sources—including solar, wind, nuclear, and hydro—accounted for 52 percent of China's total installed power capacity, surpassing coal for the first time in history, and in solar production specifically, in one year, China nearly tripled the entire installed capacity of the United States.[167]

But this dominance comes with complications that trade hawks are right to flag. As already discussed, much of China's green technology advantage stems from massive state subsidies, below-market financing, and deliberate overcapacity designed to drive out foreign competitors. The same policies that accelerated China's green transition also created market distortions that undercut manufacturers in Europe, America, and elsewhere. As the *Financial Times* noted in 2024, Chinese solar panel prices fell so far below production costs that they effectively became "subsidized dumping," forcing European manufacturers such as Meyer Burger to close facilities despite surging global demand.[168] Much of China's clean-tech capacity was built with Western orders and financing, so in essence, we outsourced not only manufacturing and pollution but the future of green industry itself.

Yes, we should be unhappy about the subsidies, the opaque financing, and the deliberate overcapacity designed to corner markets. But the capacity now exists. Gigafactories, refineries, and production lines are already built, humming, and capable of producing the very tools the planet needs to decarbonize. We can either treat this as a threat to be walled off or as an asset to be intelligently leveraged. The smart approach is not to pretend the ship hasn't sailed—it has—but to steer it toward shared goals while building our next-generation renewable fleet at home.

It's too late to argue over whether China should have built these factories or not; it's what we choose to do with these factories now. Climate change won't wait for perfect market fairness.

NATIONAL SECURITY: TRUST, SUPPLY, AND THE COST OF ALIENATING ALLIES

The loudest argument against free trade today is national security. Hawks warn that outsourcing core manufacturing to adversaries is economic madness. Former US Trade Representative Robert Lighthizer, speaking at a Peterson Institute event in 2020, declared, "You can't be a great power if you don't make things."[169] Some rhetoric goes even further, implying that each import dollar is a bullet fired at America's heart.

The passion is real, and it's not entirely misplaced.

- **COVID-19** exposed brittle supply chains when 72 percent of US hospitals reported shortages of essential personal protective equipment in April 2020.[170] The US imported over 70 percent of its medical gloves and 80 percent of its basic antibiotics from abroad, with much of that production concentrated in China and India.[171]
- **Russia's invasion of Ukraine** in 2022 highlighted the danger of energy dependence. Before the war, the European Union

imported 45 percent of its natural gas and 25 percent of its crude oil from Russia. When Moscow cut supplies, Europe faced a historic energy shock, with gas prices spiking more than 600 percent at their peak.[172]

- **China's pressure on Taiwan** has focused minds globally. The world writ large is so dependent on the advanced semiconductors Taiwan alone produces that a blockade or attack would ripple through every sector of the global economy.

Resilience in the face of a new global competitor—in trade and in political clout—matters. But the leap from "We need resilience" to "Reshore everything, tariff everyone" is a misdiagnosis.

The leap from "We need resilience" to "Reshore everything, tariff everyone" is a misdiagnosis.

First, foreign manufacturing does not automatically equal foreign control. We saw this with computer chips designed and IP'd in the US, while made in Taiwan.

Second, tariffs are a blunt weapon. They often weaken allies while barely denting adversaries. When the Trump administration imposed sweeping steel tariffs in 2018, Canada, Japan, and the EU were hit harder than China. In fact, only 3 percent of US steel imports came directly from China, while 40 percent came from Canada, Mexico, and the EU.[173] The tariffs provoked retaliatory measures that hit US agriculture especially hard. USDA and the Congressional Research Service note that farm exports to China collapsed in 2018 and 2019, forcing Washington to authorize tens of billions of dollars in emergency payments to offset lost markets.[174]

Meanwhile, China adapted. Its overall trade surplus actually grew, rising from $351 billion in 2018 to $877 billion in 2022, thanks to booming exports in sectors such as electronics and medical supplies.[175]

Third, America has one thing China does not: a network of powerful, trusted allies. Together, the US and its formal allies account for nearly 60 percent of global GDP, compared to just 6 percent for China's closest partners.[176] When America slaps tariffs indiscriminately, it undermines this network—alienating Japan, Germany, Canada, and South Korea at precisely the moment when shared strategic coordination is most needed.

THE ALLIANCE ADVANTAGE

While sitting at an airport lounge at Haneda Airport in Tokyo, I met Mr. Tanaka, a Japanese executive whose company supplies precision mechanical instruments used in making robots. His firm, family-owned, grew up inside the post-war US–Japan alliance. Then came US steel tariffs imposed under the banner of national security. Japan was hit with the same duties as China and Russia.

Mr. Tanaka told me over some whiskeys we decided to share (it was a long layover) that the financial hit hurt, but the message hurt far more. "We are your ally," he told me softly. "We host your bases. And yet you treat us no different from China." He told me many younger executives began to ask: Why remain so exposed to the US market? Why not deepen ties with China, where demand is booming?

The real national security threat is not the fate of Mr. Tanaka's steel instruments. It's the loss of Mr. Tanaka as our friend. I got him another whiskey and told him I was sorry. He shrugged and said, "What can you do?"

National security is about relationships more than it is about factories. Supply chains are not simply a network of machines and warehouses; they are a network of people tied together through transactions of trust.

When we apply tariffs indiscriminately, we send a message that is sometimes louder than the policy itself. To allies like Mr. Tanaka, the message is this: *We don't see you as a partner. We see you as a tool. Sometimes, we see you as a threat.* When friends stop feeling like friends, the bonds that hold our world together begin to fray.

The great irony is that America's deepest strategic advantage is not what we make, but who we make it with. No modern fighter jet, no aircraft carrier, no quantum chip is built entirely within one set of borders. Take the F-35 Lightning II: Its engine comes from the UK, its radar components from Italy, its landing gear from the Netherlands, and its weapons systems software from Israel.[177] This multilateral production strengthens the alliance that supports it. Every partner nation that contributes to the F-35 has a stake in American security, and America has a stake in theirs. This is the engineered brilliance of modern security: a web of interdependence that has kept the peace for eighty years.

> **When friends stop feeling like friends, the bonds that hold our world together begin to fray.**

China, by contrast, has no such network. Its closest economic partners—Russia, Iran, and North Korea—are no comparison to Japan, South Korea, and the EU. That asymmetry is our greatest weapon, and it doesn't cost us a dollar to wield it.

Why are we blowing the hell out of it?!

A smarter approach would be to coordinate with allies to address shared concerns about China's trade practices while preserving the trust that makes coordination possible. This might mean joint action on technology transfers, coordinated restrictions on sensitive exports, or shared investment in critical supply chains. What it cannot mean is treating Japan the same as Russia or Germany the same as Iran.

When Washington treats allies the same as adversaries, it weakens trust and leaves America more isolated than before. We risk losing the very thing that makes us strong: a world built on shared purpose. The point of national security is to build a world in which our friends—and their friends—stand with us.

America does not need to, nor should it try, to make everything at home. It should keep making the right things with the right friends. Because when Mr. Tanaka lifts his glass and wonders aloud if Japan should turn toward China instead, we should hear more than frustration in his voice. We should hear the faint sound of a thread unraveling, the first stitch in the fabric of security coming loose. If enough of those threads unravel, no tariff, wall, or arsenal will hold the world together.

And we will be in grave danger.

BRING
JOBS
HOME
NO
MORE
CHINA
TRADE

CHAPTER 6

THE AMERICAN WORKER

Regardless of everything I have written about the value found in trade relationships and the importance of the US's relationship with China, I still feel guilty. I have carried this guilt for most of my career.

Yes, I am an outsourcer to China. I justify my involvement because I believe free trade is good and because I saw a billion people lifted out of poverty in real time. I am happy—proud even—to have contributed to that in my small way.

But my lane in the trade game mostly ran one way: from American companies to their overseas supply chains. I have seen the dramatic upside. My business seldom required me to look the other way—toward American labor, toward the towns and counties bearing the brunt of globalization's downside.

I am not ignorant of that downside. I have heard the stories from family and friends; I have read the studies. Economist David Autor has documented what he calls the China shock: From 1999 to 2011, Chinese import competition displaced an estimated 2.4 million US jobs, leaving some towns with long-term unemployment, rising opioid addiction, and a collapse of civic life.[178] These are the numbers that US politicians point to when they rail against globalization. The statistics are hard to swallow and hard to argue against.

For years, I held these facts at arm's length. I told myself that the losses were the relatively small downside to what is a massive global good. I was aware that my gain, and the gain of many Asian friends, may have come at someone else's expense. But in the grand scheme of things—on a humanity-wide scale—it seemed to me there were more upsides than downsides, more winners than losers. Intellectually, I know the data bears this out, but deep down, I still can't shake the guilt.

If free trade is an open door that brings in sunlight and fresh air, then worker displacement is one of the nasty drafts that can also come in: A persistent chill that never completely dyes down.

So, to assuage my guilt, I went looking for the losers of trade. For the groups the pundits say were gutted by globalization: the working class, the rural Main Streets, the factory workers with hard hats in hand staring at a shuttered factory door. I wanted to see them, hear their stories, understand their lives. And not from a distance, but up close.

Having lived full-time in the US for the past four years, I was finally experiencing my own country as an adult, after more than three decades abroad. My trading business—subject to various combinations of antidumping duties, countervailing duties, and outright tariffs—had to change. While I had once led the charge into China, my partners and I were also part of the effort to move supply chains out: to Southeast Asia, to Mexico, and eventually back to the US. I traveled for work, along with those partners, sitting in bars and diners with plant managers in Pennsylvania, discussing workforce issues at industry trade shows in Illinois and Indiana, and interviewing laborers and their representatives at Texas factories. I watched production lines hum back to life in California, saw the challenges of reshoring logistics unfold in real time, and talked candidly with the people who make American industry tick.

And throughout that process, I did not find the monolithic victims the pundits claimed existed. Yes, I found individual setbacks, stories of personal disruption, and moments of struggle. But no single class, race, or occupation that had been uniformly ruined by global trade. What I encountered was disruption: broad, uneven, deeply personal, and highly localized. The impact outsourcing to China has on US workers is far more nuanced than the simplified narratives we often hear in media or political commentary.

What follows are some examples of that complexity: Stories that reflect the human texture behind trade statistics and tariff headlines.

AMBRIDGE, PENNSYLVANIA; AND EVERETT, WASHINGTON: THE ONE-COMPANY TOWNS

I spent a lot of time in Ambridge, specifically at a craft beer hall about a five-minute drive from a solar steel plant my company reshored nearby. Over delicious IPAs with the locals, I learned that Ambridge was not a town that one day attracted a factory. It was a settlement that came into being *because* of a factory. The town's very name is short for American Bridge Company, a division of US Steel, and for most of the twentieth century, it was one of the most productive steel fabrication sites in the country. Bridges, buildings, warships—all of them began as steel beams forged and riveted in Ambridge. During the town's heyday, the clang of metal and the hiss of welding torches echoed through the Ohio River valley.

But the problem with a company town is that when the company goes, the town goes too. When global steel competition ramped up, the American Bridge plant shuttered. Ambridge lost its one and only anchor. The proud workers—many of them second- or third-generation steelworkers—suddenly had nowhere to use their skills, and most moved away.

My company's solar structure plant was returning steel to the area after about three decades of absence, and we had an awful time finding labor. The steelworking skill set had largely gone extinct. The town's pain was evident to see on its streets, though it was finding a very interesting second life as a creative artist space.

Now travel across the country to Everett, Washington. My sister's toy business is headquartered just north of Everett, and many of her employees have a spouse or parent employed there. Everett also grew around a single company: Boeing. In fact, at one point, it housed the largest building by volume in the world: the Boeing Everett Site, where 747s and 787s were built. Like Ambridge, Everett's economic fate was tethered to one industrial giant.

But in Everett's case, even as Boeing rode the waves of global trade, its presence in Everett remained. The work was too specialized, its contracts too strategic to move. Much of its production was tied to long-term US defense contracts, and the company remained embedded in a regional cluster of aerospace suppliers and skilled labor. While Boeing certainly offshored parts and manufacturing, its critical operations stayed put, and so did the jobs.

When my sister drives to Seattle-Tacoma Airport for a flight to China to see her vendors, she drives past Everett and through bucolic commuter villages of unmistakable prosperity.

Everett wasn't more virtuous than Ambridge. It simply got lucky: Boeing could stay, whereas American Bridge had to close. And with that single reality came the difference between slow decay and stable growth.

PITTSBURGH AND CLEVELAND: THE TALE OF TWO STEEL CITIES

My company's US headquarters is in Pittsburgh—only thirty miles east of Ambridge. If you had driven into Pittsburgh in the early 1980s, you would have seen the same depression as in Ambridge but on a larger scale. The steel industry—the one that built the city, forged its identity, and powered the country—was collapsing under the same global weights that crushed Ambridge. Tens of thousands of jobs vanished in just a few years. The Monongahela River, once lined with barges and blast furnaces, flowed past rusted relics of America's industrial prime.

But Pittsburgh pivoted. It leaned into what the steel era had left behind: a dense network of engineers, craftsmen, and problem-solvers. It had Carnegie Mellon and the University of Pittsburgh, institutions that specialized in applied academics. Researchers who once developed stronger alloys turned to robotics, self-driving cars, and software. Medical specialists, funded by the University of Pittsburgh Medical Center's growing influence, transformed the region into a center of life sciences.

Two hours away, Cleveland tells a different story. When my parents were first married, they lived in Cleveland. At that time, it stood shoulder to shoulder with Pittsburgh: a titan of heavy manufacturing and proud home to auto parts, steelworks, and machinery. Like Pittsburgh, it had been battered by globalization. But unlike Pittsburgh, Cleveland never quite found its second act.

This wasn't for lack of assets. Case Western Reserve is a strong university. Cleveland Clinic is a world-class hospital. The Rock & Roll Hall of Fame draws tourists. But the city struggled to translate those strengths into a new economic identity. The loss of manufacturing wasn't offset by new industry. Venture capital passed on it.

Young professionals left. Cleveland still has moments of brilliance—research breakthroughs, cultural pride, deep community roots—but its economic base remains fragile.

KANSAS VERSUS IOWA: A RURAL COIN TOSS

Drive through North Central Kansas, and you will pass through towns such as Smith Center, where the signs of rural decline are subtle but unmistakable. I was in the area because there are a number of steel tube manufacturers in that part of Kansas. The grain silos still stand, the water towers still bear the town's name, and Main Street still hosts a handful of storefronts. But look closer, as I did at a dinner at Pete's BBQ, talking with a factory representative, and you'll learn that the high school football team has to combine with the teams of two other towns to fill a roster. The only grocery store closes at six at night. The hospital cut its maternity ward years ago.

Smith Center, like many rural towns in Kansas, was built around an agricultural economy that no longer exists in the form it once did. The economies of scale demanded by today's commodity markets leave little room for the family-owned midsize operator. Federal farm policy, once aimed at preserving rural vitality, has long since pivoted toward consolidation and industrial agriculture.

Now, drive a few hours northeast into Iowa, and you'll hit Storm Lake: a town that, on paper, shouldn't look all that different from Smith Center. Same rural geography. Same dependency on agriculture. Same weather and distance from the coasts. I was there because Storm Lake not only hosts several steel fabrication facilities but is also a logistics hub for suppliers accessing the Upper Midwest. There was a vitality in the town that was entirely missing from Smith Center.

Storm Lake has held on to its vitality, like Pittsburgh, by absorbing change. The Tyson meatpacking plant brought jobs. Those jobs brought immigrants: from Guatemala, Laos, Mexico, and Somalia. Those immigrants brought children. And those children brought life. The schools are growing. The churches are full, some offering services in three languages. On a walk down Main Street, I was surprised to see Vietnamese grocers and taco trucks parked next to hardware stores. It's not the America most nostalgic political ads display.

Or is it?

Maybe the faces are just different. It was not that long ago that the Irish, the Polish, and the Scandinavians were the new faces.

Ambridge, Cleveland, and Smith Center are not struggling because their people lack pride or work ethic. They're behind because their economies were built around fixed structures: single employers, legacy industries, inherited systems that didn't pivot when the global influences crashed in. Meanwhile, Everett, Pittsburgh, and Storm Lake found ways to revamp, making them able to absorb disruption and to thrive.

INDIVIDUALS, NOT SLOGANS

Let's zoom in further—past cities and towns—and look at people.

Darrell worked the blast furnaces in Johnstown for Bethlehem Steel, just as his father had. He was a union representative, proud of negotiating better dental coverage and safer conditions. But when the mill finally collapsed in 1993, none of that mattered. Darrell's pension froze. Trade Adjustment Assistance, a few years later, sent him to a six-week web design course in a county with no broadband at that time. It was policy theater, not help.

Years later, Darrell drove to see our solar steel plant, where his son worked as a quality engineer. He stood quietly on the shop floor, watching the lines move. He didn't trust that steel jobs could last. Experience had taught him otherwise.

Then there was Mike, a third-generation metalworker from the same region. When his fabrication plant closed in the early 2000s, most of the union workers took buyouts or warehouse jobs. Mike took a loan instead. He bought a few used CNC machines, set them up in a garage behind his house, and started fabricating components himself. He plugged into a global supply chain, partnering with a South Korean firm supplying a unique bracket to an electric bike plant one state over. When we met over craft beers, he was planning his first trip to Busan and wanted advice.

Same region. Same shock. Two radically different outcomes.

AUTOMATION'S SHADOW

I was in Laramie, Wyoming learning more about the huge wind investments in an area with one of the strongest, most consistent wind resources in the country.

I met Eugene at Lovejoy's Bar & Grill. He previously was a logistics warehouse clerk in Cheyenne. Now he was looking to reinvent himself. He didn't lose his job to a foreign country. He lost it to robotic handling, digitization, and an Amazon logistics hub. Even as the movement of goods grew busier at Cheyenne's crossroads of two major interstate highways, Eugene was pushed out. The work didn't disappear; the people did. Maybe a University of Wyoming's off-campus certificate program might help him.

A 2015 study by economists at Ball State University found that productivity gains—automation—eliminated 5.6 million manufacturing jobs between 2000 and 2010, with trade only accounting for about 13 percent of the decline.[179] Trade got the blame because factory closures are visible and emotionally resonant, while productivity gains happen gradually and invisibly.

The next night I met Cody, a heavy equipment operator from Gillette, Wyoming, who was in Laramie for his cousin's wedding. Cody didn't have a college degree, but he knew rocks. He came up through coal. When global energy markets shifted and coal lost favor, he and a handful of former coworkers moved into sodium bentonite clay. Wyoming supplies a dominant share of the world's known bentonite reserves into global markets, with rising demand from Asia and the Middle East. Cody was always busy, barely finding time to make his cousin's wedding party.

Loss, adaptation, reinvention. The line between them is thin.

MAIN STREET: GONE OR TRANSFORMED?

I met Carl and Janice when I was a third wheel crashing a friend's family reunion. They were former owners of a home-goods store in rural Missouri. Carl's father opened it in 1958. You could buy a hammer, a coffeepot, and a birthday card in one stop. They sponsored Little League. They donated to church raffles. They were Main Street.

Then Walmart arrived. Carl couldn't buy nails wholesale for what Walmart sold retail. He knew why: Tianjin, Guangdong, Bangladesh. The store closed in 2009 after fifty-one years. Now they watch their grandkids so the family can avoid daycare costs.

Contrast that with Lisa, a fifth-generation farmer near Ames, Iowa. I met her at the China International Agricultural Trade Fair, where she was promoting American soybeans. She modernized her farm with GPS planting and moisture sensors, learned USDA export protocols, tracked futures prices in Shanghai, and leaned into Asia's growing appetite for protein. Global markets made her richer than anyone in her rural family had ever been.

Same economy. Same region, and even the same political leanings. Different outcomes.

THE PATTERN

I think you see where I'm going. It's tempting to say the working class lost or that Main Street died. But that's not quite what happened. Some people did lose. Some areas did die. But others did not. Others thrived.

There is no single, monolithic American hinterland. No great trade gash across a uniformly bleeding American chest. There are indeed areas where deep wounds exist, where the negative aspects of trade are concentrated, but they sit next to other areas where trade was beneficial: Sometimes two towns, one doing well, one not, sitting next to each other in the same county. In short, there is a patchwork of highly individualized stories scattered across the map, each shaped by its own mix of luck, timing, and resilience.

There is no single, monolithic American hinterland. No great trade gash across a uniformly bleeding American chest.

THE CHINA SHOCK

David Autor's research helps explain the unevenness running through these stories. His findings are nuanced in ways that both trade critics and advocates often ignore.

Yes, Chinese import competition displaced 2.4 million US jobs between 1999 and 2011. But context matters: In an economy with over 150 million workers, this amounts to roughly 200,000 jobs per year, or about 0.13 percent of the workforce annually. The disruption was real but scattered. It was hardly a national collapse.

Autor's work reveals something further. When researchers trace not only direct competition (Chinese goods displacing US-made goods) but also upstream suppliers and downstream users of imported inputs, the picture changes. Firms that could tap cheaper, higher-quality components often expanded output, moved into new product lines, and hired for nonmanufacturing roles in logistics, marketing, design, IT, and customer service. In some estimates, these downstream gains were large enough across the whole economy to offset (and occasionally exceed) the direct and upstream manufacturing losses. The winners, in other words, certainly existed.

They were just harder to see.

There's another hidden upside: welfare effects. Even Autor acknowledges gains beyond job counts. For instance, economic gains can include lower consumer prices, greater variety in goods, and efficiency improvements that raise real purchasing power. Cheaper inputs and goods free up household income and business capital, which then spill into restaurants, hospitals, construction sites, and service firms far from the factory floor. Quantifying exactly how many jobs those indirect benefits create is hard—and imprecise—but they are part of the honest ledger.

None of this is to minimize the pain of communities hit by this China shock. Their losses are real and worthy of empathy and response. But we should resist turning that pain into a sweeping slogan. The fuller picture shows a patchwork of effects: concentrated harm, diffuse gains, and significant consumer benefits.

Then there is a huge, separate shock hitting workers from automation.

Yes, China was a shock. But it was one shock among many.

THE OTHER SIDE OF THE MIRROR: CHINA'S SHOCK

The unevenness I saw across the United States did not originate in America, nor was it unique to it. The same forces that dislocated workers in Ambridge and Smith Center tore through China—only faster, harder, and at far greater scale.

Ms. Zhang, fifty-eight, is the only person left in her village in rural Gansu province. Her children live in cities—one of them in Shanghai, employed at a logistics company I worked with. Her husband died years ago while working on a construction site in Shenzhen. Once, her village had thirty families, fields full of wheat, and a communal rhythm. Now, it has overgrown paths and padlocked doors.

When China embraced globalization, millions of citizens like Ms. Zhang were left behind. Between 1990 and 2015, more than three hundred million rural Chinese migrated to cities—the largest human migration in history.[180] Global trade made village-based agriculture unprofitable. It pulled the young away and left the old behind.

Mrs. Li, from rural Sichuan, represents the migrants who left. She moved to Dongguan in the early 2000s to work in a toy factory that supplied parts to my sister's business. She sewed doll clothes for twelve hours a day, six days a week. The factory didn't allow children in the dorms, so her son was raised by his grandparents. She saw him once a year during the Chinese New Year holidays.

American critics often call workers like Mrs. Li slave laborers, but that notion misses the complexity of her choice. Mrs. Li lined up outside the Dongguan factory for days to get this job because the wages, while low by US standards, were transformational by Chinese village standards. She lived in factory dorms, ate in mess halls, and wired her savings home for her son's betterment. He might go to university, something no one in her village had ever done.

Compare Mrs. Li's story to Mr. Wang's. Mr. Wang worked for a state-owned steel mill in Shenyang—China's equivalent of the rust belt cities of America. His concerned son told me about him over dinner. His father was a Party member; his uncle had fought in Korea. Mr. Wang thought his job was secure. The work wasn't glamorous, but it came with benefits: housing, pensions, the so-called iron rice bowl: the old communist idea of providing basic security for life. Then, in the early 2000s, the mill shut down. It couldn't compete with private exporters in the more entrepreneurial cities of Wuhan, Suzhou, and Shanghai. Mr. Wang was laid off at forty-seven. No retraining, no severance. He drifted between gig work and depression. His son wanted to know if I knew any suppliers who might hire him.

China's reform and opening meant privatizing inefficient state firms. By some estimates, over forty million workers (a number greater than the population of California) were laid off because of restructuring in the late 1990s and early 2000s.[181] The number of job losses of American workers seems almost mild by comparison.

Yes, trade lifted hundreds of millions in China out of poverty, but not without casualties. And like in America, the gains were wide-ranging and diffused throughout the population, while the wounds were concentrated in certain towns and villages. Global trade affected China's population haphazardly, individually. Trade rewarded mobility, adaptability, and access to capital. It punished stasis, economic routine, and rootedness. Like in the US, the people who could pivot—whether by education, geography, or sheer luck—mostly did fine. But those whose identities were wrapped up in a place, a factory, or a specific industry did worse.

This symmetry matters.

American workers did not lose alone. Chinese workers did not win uniformly. Global trade did not divide the world into villains and victims. It reshaped societies haphazardly, leaving scars that policymakers on both sides still struggle to address.

LEFT AND RIGHT SEE THE SAME SICKNESS

Peter Navarro, Trump's trade czar, paints global trade—especially with China—as a calculated assault on American workers and national security. (Remember the hemorrhage and the notion that the US is the world's biggest trade loser?) His approach frames trade not as mutual exchange but as zero-sum warfare, calling for steep tariffs and repatriation of supply chains to restore US manufacturing.[182]

While Ambridge, Cleveland, and Smith Center might agree, Everett, Pittsburgh, and Storm Lake would disagree.

Senator Bernie Sanders has long argued that trade deals have systematically harmed American workers. He famously suggested that these trade agreements were going to destroy the middle class. He opposed NAFTA, the Dominican Republic–Central America Free Trade Agreement, permanent normal trade relations with China, and the Trans-Pacific Partnership (TPP), calling them "disastrous trade agreements."[183] Sanders frames trade not as mutually beneficial, but as fueling a race to the bottom that undermines wages, labor rights, and middle-class stability.

While Darrell, Eugene, Carl, and Janice might have screamed in support at a Bernie Sanders fundraiser, Mike, Cody, and Lisa would have rolled their eyes at home and flipped the channel.

Both Navarro and Sanders saw real pain in American communities, and they weren't wrong about the suffering. But they misdiagnosed its source.

China's rise was not a conspiracy or a policy blunder. It was a demographic shock: A fifth of humanity reentering the global economy after generations of enforced isolation. That kind of shift bends wages, redirects capital, and rearranges entire industrial systems. No country absorbs a change of that scale smoothly or evenly.

I recognize my own role in that story, and my luck in it. By accident of birth—being raised in Taiwan, learning Mandarin young—I stood on lucky ground. I benefited from that shock in ways families in Ambridge and Cleveland never could. They absorbed costs they didn't choose and couldn't escape. I soaked in wins I had almost nothing to do with creating. The contrast has never sat comfortably with me.

But guilt, by itself, is not a policy. And it is not an argument against trade.

Before we turn disruption into doctrine, we have to look honestly at what trade created: Who gained, who lost, and where responsibility truly lies.

That requires an honest reading of the ledger.

THE HONEST TRADE LEDGER

In 1981, over 40 percent of the world lived in extreme poverty, defined as living on less than $2.15 per day. By 2019, that number had fallen to less than 9 percent.[184] That's more than one billion people lifted from destitution. China alone went from having 85 percent in extreme poverty in 1981 to virtually 0 percent living in poverty by 2020.[185]

Vietnam has followed a similar path. Since opening its economy in the 1990s and embracing exports, Vietnam's poverty rate has dropped from over 70 percent to under 6 percent.[186] Today, 30 percent of Vietnamese jobs are tied to exports.

According to the World Bank, "No country has grown to middle-income status without integrating into the global trading system."[187]

Export-oriented firms in developing countries pay, on average, 16 percent higher wages than their domestically focused counterparts.[188]

In India, Ethiopia, Sri Lanka ... a similar pattern plays out. Jobs created through global outsourcing, while paying modest wages by Western standards, represent life-changing opportunities in their local contexts.

And what about the US?

Trade translated into staggering gains. Firms tapped into low-cost manufacturing abroad, dramatically lowered their cost structures, and scaled globally in ways that would have been unimaginable in a closed economy. American corporations offshored production, yes, but retained control of branding, design, finance, and intellectual property. The result was a windfall of corporate profits and a stock market boom that far outpaced that of global peers. By 2020, US equities accounted for nearly two-thirds of total global stock market capitalization, an astonishing leap from just one-quarter of global capitalization in the 1980s.[189]

Meanwhile, trade acted as a powerful deflationary force. China's entry into the WTO in 2001 alone reduced US consumer prices by 1 to 1.5 percent across a broad basket of goods.[190] Without trade, the Federal Reserve would have had to raise interest rates much higher to tame inflation. Instead, Americans got flat-screen TVs, smartphones, clothes, and toys at prices that often fell even as wages stagnated.

A billion people leaving poverty is not an abstraction. It's a miracle.

It's a chance at an education instead of child labor. Chicken and rice instead of boiled weeds. Opportunity instead of stasis.

Trade works.

But, yes, the ledger remains incomplete.

THE REAL DIAGNOSIS

Peter Navarro and Bernie Sanders, as different as they are, both saw a sickness. And they weren't entirely wrong. Factories did close. Wages did stagnate. Some communities hollowed out.

But they were wrong about the cause.

The disease wasn't trade. It was hoarded gains.

While the towns of Ambridge and Smith Center struggled to survive, the gains from global trade were captured by far too few. In the very years the China shock hit hardest, US corporate profits reached record highs. In 2018 alone, as communities such as those David Autor studied were still recovering from decades of manufacturing job losses, S&P 500 companies initiated $800 billion in stock buybacks.[191]

That same year, the TAA—the program designed to help workers such as Darrell transition to new careers—received just $800 million.[192] The US spent as much in twelve months rewarding shareholders as it allocated in an entire decade to retraining displaced workers. To put this in perspective, by my calculations using readily available data, that $800 billion could have funded the establishment of four thousand new community colleges, each serving five thousand students, or provided $320,000 in retraining and transition support to every one of the 2.4 million workers displaced by the China shock.

> **The US spent as much in twelve months rewarding shareholders as it allocated in an entire decade to retraining displaced workers.**

But no, we chose share buybacks.

That imbalance was reinforced by corporate tax policy. While manufacturing towns watched their local tax bases erode, the companies benefiting from global supply chains used schemes such as the Double Irish with a Dutch Sandwich (a legal tax avoidance strategy used by multinational corporations to move profits from high-tax countries to low- or no-tax jurisdictions) to shift $2.6 trillion in profits offshore, avoiding $750 billion in US taxes.[193] Those missing tax revenues could have funded massive infrastructure renewal, education programs, and economic development in precisely the communities hit hardest by trade.

In China, the hoarding happened differently but with similar effects. The Communist Party clamped down on capital outflows, creating the "unbalanced balance" that Michael Pettis described. Export earnings that should have circulated freely through society, and back to the United States, were instead funneled into state-owned enterprises, infrastructure megaprojects, and geopolitical ventures.

We compounded that failure by abandoning solid trade partners. Instead of reinforcing rule-based trade with allies, we walked away from the Trans-Pacific Partnership, a pact covering 40 percent of global GDP and embedding labor rights, digital trade rules, and limits on state-owned enterprises. Our allies stayed in it. We left. China has since applied to join.

In its place, we turned to blunt-force tariffs, slapping duties on allies and adversaries alike. In 2018 alone, American consumers and manufacturers paid $21 billion more for steel and aluminum, while allies retaliated and China adapted with ease.

That's what you call self-inflicted damage.

Other countries show that different choices were possible. Denmark's flexicurity system combines labor market flexibility with robust social protection. Workers can be laid off easily, but they receive generous unemployment benefits, extensive retraining, and help finding new jobs. The result is one of the world's most dynamic economies with one of the lowest unemployment rates. Germany pairs export success with strong worker representation through codetermination laws that give employees seats on corporate boards that consider worker interests alongside shareholder returns. These weren't accidents. They were policy choices: investments in institutions that could manage disruption rather than letting it fester. America had more than enough resources to make similar choices. We just chose to let them pool at the top instead of circulating (at least some) through the communities that needed them most.

The shock wasn't that trade created winners and losers—that's inevitable with any major economic disruption. The shock was that we had the resources to help the losers but chose not to use them. The shock was that in the richest country in human history, we told displaced steelworkers there wasn't enough money for retraining while spending close to a trillion dollars rewarding shareholders for corporate financial engineering.

Understanding this correct diagnosis is the first step toward a cure. Trade wasn't the enemy of the American worker; abandonment was. The policies we need to craft as a nation today are not ones that curtail trade, but ones that address our decades of systemic neglect of those most vulnerable to disruption—any disruption.

MY JUST REWARDS

At the end of the day, I must own my guilt.

I think about Darrell—the steelworker whose entire town emptied out while distant shareholders got richer. I helped make that happen. Not directly, not intentionally, but I was part of the machinery. I spent years optimizing supply chains, finding the cheapest factory, negotiating the tightest margins, and delivering the quarterly wins to Darrell's bosses that Wall Street rewarded and Darrell had to pay for.

I helped corporations save billions but said nothing when they spent those savings on stock buybacks. I helped Chinese factories scale to unimaginable size and never asked what happened to the capital they earned: how it was trapped, distorted, weaponized by a state that refused to let it flow freely.

I believed that if we made trade efficient enough, cheap enough, fast enough, prosperity would find its way to everyone eventually.

I was wrong about that.

For a long time, I told myself this wasn't my problem. Even Deng Xiaoping said that some people had to get rich first. I was just the logistician. The middleman. Someone else set policy; someone else distributed the gains. My job was to make the system work, not to question how the gains were distributed.

But systems don't happen by accident. They are built by choices—millions of them, compounded over decades. Every time I optimized a supply chain without asking what happened to the workers displaced by it, I made a choice. Every time I celebrated cost savings without questioning where those savings went, I made a choice. Every time I stayed silent while shareholders extracted a trillion dollars that could have rebuilt communities, retrained workers, and renewed the promise that trade would lift everyone—I made a choice.

I know what those choices cost now.

I still believe in free trade—more than ever. I believe it is one of the great moral achievements of the modern world. But a system that lets gains pool at the top while losses concentrate below is not sustainable. It will not hold. And it will not survive politically, no matter how strong its economic logic.

Guilt, though, is passive. It sits heavy in your chest and points backward.

Responsibility points forward.

I can't restore the mills in Ambridge or rebuild Main Street in Smith Center. But I can name what went wrong. I can reject the easy villain narratives. And I can argue—clearly, repeatedly, and without apology—that the next chapter of global trade must be written differently.

We need policies that don't just open markets but also recycle gains.

We need companies that don't just maximize profit but also invest in people.

We need a system that values financial efficiency right alongside community resilience.

Because the alternative is already visible: rising nationalism, collapsing trust, and a slow retreat from the very system that created unprecedented global wealth in the first place.

This book is my first step toward confronting that truth. It won't be my last.

If you worked in a factory that closed, if you lost a job to forces you didn't choose, if you watched your town weaken while markets soared—I see you. I'm sorry I didn't see you sooner.

I'll spend the rest of my career trying to build something better.

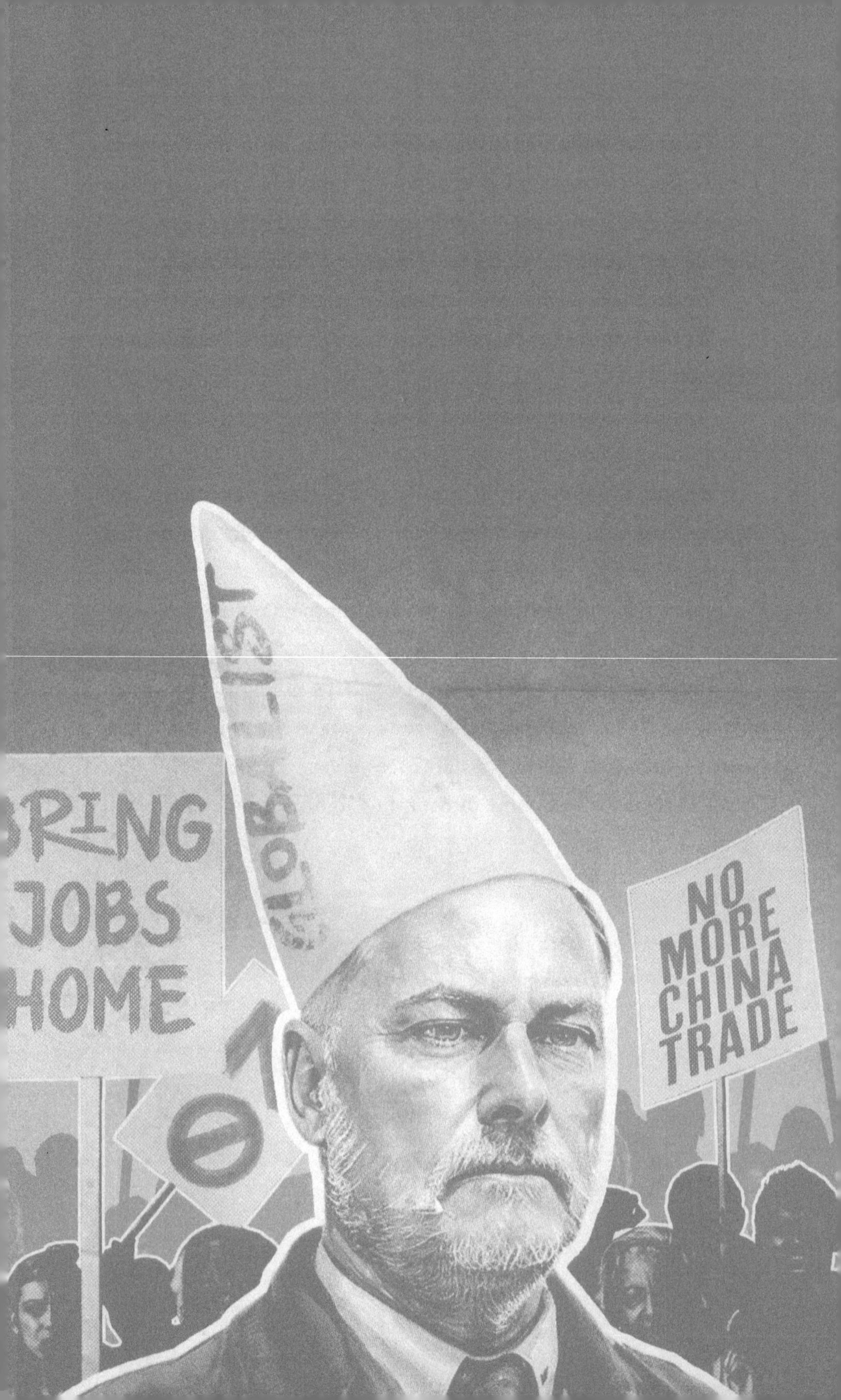

JOBS
NO MORE CHINA TRADE

PART III

WHAT HAPPENS NOW?

明察秋毫

(Ming cha qiu hao)

To perceive the finest hair even in autumn colors.

BRING
JOBS
HOME
NO
MORE
CHINA
TRADE

CHAPTER 7

TARIFFS AND THE FUTILITY OF PROTECTION

While most economists (and most businesspeople) believe that trade has benefited far more people than it has hurt, the politics of this moment has latched only onto the hurt. And elections seem to be fought today based on who can be the toughest on free trade in general, and on China in particular.

This runs counter to eighty years of American consensus that has upheld free trade. We used to tell the world that markets work best when barriers come down, when goods flow freely across borders, when competition drives efficiency. That was the language we used in Geneva at the WTO, in bilateral trade talks, and in op-eds about the virtues of globalization.

But it seems our faith in free trade has been shaken. Suddenly, free trade is no longer a universal wealth-creating principle but dangerous because we have seen disruptions … as if our economy has never seen a disruption before. The political reflex to this anxiety is tariffs, quotas, duties, "safeguards." Politicians promise to bring back jobs, punish foreign competitors, and restore American manufacturing. With very short memories, we dust off the protectionist tools of the Smoot-Hawley Act and tell ourselves it is temporary, defensive, or simply "fair."

But they don't work. Protectionism has never worked.

That tension—between the rhetoric of openness and the sudden reflexes of protection—has defined US trade policy for more than a century. When it suits us, we preach liberalization. When it's perceived to hurt us, we practice restriction. And all too often, behind the rhetoric around protectionism there is a company or an industry using its political influence to game the system, to have restrictions put in place to protect its business while turning a blind eye to the damage often done to the economy at large.

Protectionism has never worked.

Let's look at how this works in practice, starting with an obscure trade dispute that taught me everything I needed to know about tariffs. I learned this contradiction early in my career from a very strange trade fight over certain mechanical fittings. (I'm being vague because the cases are still ongoing and sensitive to my customers.)

In the late 1990s and early 2000s, the US government slapped antidumping duties on these metal fittings from China that are used in urban infrastructure. They are not particularly high-tech, but they are critical for utilities, and the margins are thin.

At the time, my family was helping a US customer source much of its production of these products from China through our networks. We had built efficient supply chains and cut costs and were reliably serving the utilities that depended on these parts. The trading relationship was working well, delivering exactly the kind of global trade efficiency the textbooks praise.

Then came the antidumping petition. A US competitor filed a case with the Department of Commerce and the International Trade Commission claiming that these parts were being dumped in the

American market—that is, sold at unfairly low prices—and that this was destroying American jobs. On paper, it looked like a patriotic defense of US industry. The argument was that Chinese imports were undercutting domestic production and threatening livelihoods and needed to be disciplined with duties.

The reality, as we discovered, was very different.

The competitor that filed the petition—loudly waving the flag of "protecting American jobs"—was making only some of the parts in the US. Its supply chain ran through Mexico. It was not fighting for American jobs; it was fighting for market share.[194] This competitor used the blunt instrument of US trade law to kneecap a rival who happened to be sourcing in China instead of Mexico.

I remember thinking at the time: This isn't economics; it isn't even about jobs. This is a commercial back-alley brawl dressed up as trade policy.

That lesson has stayed with me. Show me a tariff, and I'll show you a company with a great legal team and some good lobbyists working to gain a commercial advantage by attempting to rig the rules of the market.

WHY TARIFFS SOUND REASONABLE

While I maintain that tariffs are often (mostly?) a cynical corporate play, the arguments for them are rooted in real anxieties and can seem reasonable. Proponents will point to three main justifications.

First is the infant industry argument: that new strategic domestic industries need temporary protection to scale up and compete globally. Alexander Hamilton made this case in his 1791 book *Report on Manufactures*.[195] Developing countries, from South

Korea to Taiwan, used targeted protection to nurture industries that later became globally competitive.

Second is the issue of national security: the belief that a country shouldn't depend on a potential adversary for critical goods such as steel, semiconductors, or medical supplies. This isn't always paranoia. As explained, the COVID-19 pandemic exposed dangerous dependencies on Chinese production for masks, ventilators, and pharmaceutical ingredients. China's control over critical minerals used in defense systems represents a genuine security vulnerability. There are narrow cases—perhaps advanced microchips for missile guidance systems or certain rare earth elements with no substitutes—in which accepting higher costs to maintain domestic capacity might be justified.

But even then, tariffs are the wrong tool. If a specific component is truly critical to national defense, the government should subsidize domestic production directly, fund research into alternatives, or maintain strategic stockpiles. Tariffs are too blunt: They raise costs across entire industries, invite retaliation, and often fail to achieve the security goal because supply chains simply reroute through third countries. The national security card gets played far too often, stretched to cover industries with tenuous connections to defense, and it almost always ends up as cover for corporate protection rather than genuine security policy.

Tariffs are too blunt: They raise costs across entire industries, invite retaliation, and often fail to achieve the security goal because supply chains simply reroute through third countries.

Then, third, there is the most common argument: leveling a playing field tilted by another country's unfair practices, such as state subsidies, intellectual property theft, or currency manipulation. When China props up industries with cheap state loans and demands technology transfer from foreign companies, the complaint that this distorts competition is legitimate.

These arguments sound reasonable. In some cases, targeted and temporary tariffs may deliver helpful economic outcomes. The problem is that tariffs never remain targeted or temporary. Hamilton's infant industries that he sought to protect in 1791 were supposed to grow up and compete, but protected industries rarely wean themselves off protection.

Take US sugar: Protection started in 1789 as a revenue tariff, and then shifted to industry protection in 1890, and which has continued for over 230 years. Rather than becoming competitive, the industry became dependent on import quotas and tariffs for protection and on the politically powerful for additional cover. Fewer than 4,200 sugar farms now account for 33 percent of all crop industry campaign donations. There are over two million American farms, so that's 0.21 percent of crop growers accounting for one-third of all crop-growing campaign donations. Yikes! And American consumers pay artificially inflated prices. The protection became so extreme that The Coca-Cola Company and PepsiCo abandoned sugar entirely in 1984, switching to high fructose corn syrup instead.

That's not an infant industry that grew up; that's an industry that is a permanent ward of the state.

As the mechanical fitting story showed me, these sometimes noble justifications for trade protection quickly become cover for something far more mundane: ensuring easy market share.

THE WASHER TARIFFS: PAYING MORE FOR LESS

Consider washing machines. In January 2018, the Trump administration imposed global tariffs on imported washers. The logic was straightforward: Protect Whirlpool Corporation from South Korean and Chinese imports, and jobs would follow.

What happened instead? Prices jumped. Washing machines cost about 12 percent more and—strangely—clothes dryer prices went up by the same amount, even though dryers weren't tariffed.[196] Retailers and manufacturers, sensing a captive market, simply raised prices across the laundry aisle. Families buying appliances absorbed the hit.

How many jobs were created? A modest 1,800 positions. Consumers, meanwhile, paid an estimated $1.5 billion extra in that first year.[197] Do the math, and it works out to over $800,000 per job created via the tariff.

Now pause on that figure. A typical American production worker in a washer plant earns about $19–$24 an hour, or roughly $40,000–$50,000 per year in wages. Even adding benefits, the total compensation might reach $60,000 annually. So, in one year, American households collectively spent more than ten times a worker's annual salary just to "buy" that job into existence. If you stretched the math over a decade, the worker might earn half a million dollars. Consumers had already shelled out more than that in the first year alone.

So, where did the rest go? It didn't flow into paychecks. Manufacturers pocketed a windfall. Whirlpool got the protection it wanted, but LG and Samsung—which were the targets—also raised prices once tariffs leveled the playing field. Retailers marked up prices in tandem. When the wholesale price rose, big-box stores such as Home Depot and Lowe's took their cut. The government collected some tariff revenue, but only a fraction of the total financial burden put on American consumers. In other words, the burden landed on American families, and the gains flowed mostly to corporations, with the workers getting only a meager sliver.

To me, that feels more like a ransom. Imagine what $1.5 billion could have done if invested directly in job training, community colleges, or infrastructure projects.

STEEL AND ALUMINUM: A TAX ON THE SUPPLY CHAIN

Steel tariffs are political dynamite. The image of molten furnaces, sparks flying, and hard hats is etched into America's industrial psyche. In 2018, again under Trump, the US imposed 25 percent tariffs on steel and 10 percent tariffs on aluminum, citing national security. In 2025, the aluminum tariff was raised to 25 percent.

At first glance, the policy seemed to work. US steel prices rose about 9 percent, and mills posted higher profits. For plants that had been struggling, it was a lifeline. Analysts estimate the tariffs may have saved or created around 8,700 jobs in the steel industry.[198]

But steel is not an end product; it's a feedstock. It flows into cars, farm equipment, construction, pipelines, appliances, and machinery. Every American manufacturer that bends, welds, or bolts metal together had to pay more for its feedstock. Ford reported that the tariffs cost the company about $1 billion in a single year. Caterpillar, General Motors, and countless midsize firms faced the same squeeze.

And here's the arithmetic: The cost per steel job saved has been pegged at around $650,000.[199] Compare that to the average steelworker's annual pay of $60,000–$70,000 in wages, maybe $80,000–$90,000 with benefits. Consumers and steel-using firms spent ten years of salary just to "buy" one job into existence in the first year.

As with the washing machine tariffs, steel producers reaped most of the gains. Tariffs gave them pricing power. Domestic mills charged more because imports were penalized, boosting profits even as overall employment barely moved. Shareholders benefited. Many steel companies used the windfall for dividends and stock buybacks. The federal government collected tariff revenue, but the amount was only a fraction of what businesses and consumers paid in higher prices.

The real losers were the downstream industries—the auto plants in Michigan, the machine shops in Ohio, the construction firms everywhere—that employ far more people than steel mills do. According to Bureau of Labor Statistics data, US iron and steel mills and ferroalloy production employ under one hundred thousand workers, while broad downstream steel-using industries (autos, metal fabrication, machinery, construction equipment) amount to several million jobs. The implication is clear: Steel producers are few, but their product touches a much wider workforce—something like a forty-to-one ratio. For every steel job protected, dozens—if not hundreds—of jobs in steel-consuming industries were put at risk.

THE TIRE TARIFFS: BIG WIN FOR THIRD-PARTY COUNTRIES

A tariff is like a giant rock on a stormy beach: You just don't know how the tide will flow around it.

Go back to 2009. The Obama administration imposed a "safeguard" tariff on Chinese car and light truck tires meant to save American jobs in Akron and elsewhere. Chinese tire exports to the US collapsed, exactly as planned. But the United States didn't win.

Other foreign suppliers—South Korea, Thailand, and Mexico—rushed to fill the gap. Imports from those countries surged, often at higher prices. US tire companies didn't expand production capacity; they didn't need to. The tariff gave everyone cover to raise prices, so they simply rode the wave.

The result? Consumers paid about $1.1 billion more for tires in the first year alone. Jobs saved? Roughly 1,200.[200] That works out to about $900,000 per job.

In effect, China lost market share, but Akron didn't gain it. Seoul, Bangkok, and Monterrey did. The US consumer got stuck with the bill, while foreign competitors pocketed much of the reward. Like with steel, tires are not where the employment action is. US tire manufacturing directly employs around fifty thousand people. The auto industry as a whole (assembly, parts, and dealerships) employs over nine hundred thousand people.

What was sold as a patriotic defense of US industry was, in reality, a shell game: China out, other countries in, consumers poorer, US auto industry put at risk, American jobs still flat.

HARLEY-DAVIDSON: TARIFFS THAT SEND JOBS ABROAD

Sometimes, tariffs even push American jobs away.

That was the story with Harley-Davidson. When the US imposed tariffs on steel and aluminum, the European Union struck back with retaliatory duties on iconic American products, including motorcycles. For Harley, this was no small matter: Europe was one of its largest markets, often rivaling or surpassing US sales and accounting for nearly 40 percent of its total market.[201] Suddenly, the cost of a Harley in Europe jumped by thousands of dollars. The company faced a choice: Lose sales abroad or adjust its production footprint. It chose the rational path. Harley announced that it would shift some manufacturing for its European market to Thailand, a move designed to keep its bikes price-competitive and preserve its distribution channels overseas.[202]

Tariffs force supply chains to reorganize around them. If the US raises barriers, firms will shift jobs, sourcing, and assembly somewhere else to keep global markets open.

For Harley, Europe was a major engine of expansion. Protecting that market meant offshoring jobs that would otherwise have remained in the US. A policy branded "America First" ended up exporting American jobs to protect one of America's most iconic brands abroad.

WHAT THE DATA SAYS

Across washers, steel, tires, and motorcycles, the pattern is consistent.

- **Tariffs raise prices sharply.** Not just on targeted goods but also on related products as manufacturers and retailers adjust pricing across entire product lines.[203,204]
- **Jobs created are minimal and costly.** Peterson Institute studies show that the average cost per job saved through tariffs exceeds $500,000–$900,000.[205,206] Compare that to job-training programs costing tens of thousands per worker or community college programs that prepare workers for modern manufacturing jobs.
- **Downstream industries foot the bill.** For every steel job saved, dozens of jobs in auto manufacturing, construction, and machinery are threatened by higher input costs.[207]
- **Supply chains reorganize.** Block China, and Vietnam or Mexico steps in. Some tariff revenue goes to Washington, but the jobs don't come home. Often, that tariff revenue must be spent to shore up industries hit by retaliatory tariffs, such as US soybeans.

Unfortunately, the data is clear. As good as imposing tariffs might feel, tariffs are not pro-worker; they are anti-consumer. And consumers are workers too. The money extracted from families buying washing machines or cars is money not spent on education, healthcare, or savings. It's a hidden tax that falls hardest on those who can least afford it.

Anyone who is pro-tariff can only be labeled pro-tax because that is the net effect of tariffs in action. And it is not "tax the rich"; it is very much a taxing of the consumer classes.

AUTOMATION AND DEMOGRAPHICS

Even in the rare cases in which tariffs or subsidies lead to factory ribbon cuttings, the workforce inside bears little resemblance to the one promised in campaign speeches. The political rhetoric evokes an image of the mid-twentieth-century unionized American worker returning to the assembly line. The reality is profoundly different.

First, as mentioned, automation dominates. A modern factory is a marvel of efficiency, run by robots and sophisticated software. While a plant in 1975 employed 1,000 people, its modern equivalent might employ 150, and most of those employees are technicians and engineers, not assembly workers. Reshoring studies consistently show that companies invest heavily in robotics to offset higher US wages. Higher input costs from tariffs only accelerate this trend, as companies seek any possible way to reduce labor expenses.

Second, the demographics of the workforce have fundamentally shifted. According to the Bureau of Labor Statistics, Hispanic workers now constitute nearly 20 percent of the entire US labor force, but their share in manufacturing and production roles is significantly higher.[208] I personally have never walked a factory floor in the US in which the main language of communication wasn't Spanish. This isn't criticism or social commentary; it's a demographic fact. The idea that tariffs will bring back a specific type of job for a specific type of worker from a bygone era ignores the technological and demographic reality of America in 2025.

Protectionist policies subsidize a highly automated, demographically diverse sector while claiming to resurrect a past that is gone forever. The factories that do reopen because of tariffs produce fewer goods with fewer workers at higher costs, precisely the opposite of what made American manufacturing dominant in the first place.

Tariffs **misunderstand supply chains.** Modern production is global and impossibly complex. A single iPhone contains components from a dozen countries. Block China, and companies shift to Vietnam, India, or Mexico. They don't rebuild in Ohio. The supply chain fragments but doesn't reshore. And in the process, it becomes less efficient and more expensive.

- **Tariffs overestimate the role of labor.** Labor is a shrinking share of manufacturing costs. In modern factories, it's often under 10 percent. And in turn, manufacturing is a shrinking share of the total American economy—also around 10 percent. Tariffs make imported inputs more expensive, which accelerates automation use rather than hiring. Companies invest in robots, not workers. A robot doesn't need health insurance, doesn't take vacations, and doesn't file workers' compensation claims.
- Tariffs **ignore who pays.** Tariffs are taxes on Americans, both consumers and businesses. Every tariff is a transfer of wealth from diffuse consumers to concentrated producers (those companies with lawyers and lobbyists).
- **Tariffs invite retaliation.** Trading partners don't sit still. They hit back at politically sensitive American exports: soybeans

> from Iowa, whiskey from Kentucky, motorcycles from Wisconsin. Farmers and manufacturers who had nothing to do with the original dispute become collateral damage in someone else's trade war.

Tariffs endure because they feel like we're being tough on competitors. Politicians can say, "We're fighting for our workers." This plays well at rallies. It sounds decisive.

But it is an illusion.

THE CHINA TARIFF FEVER DREAM

Nowhere has this failure been more spectacular, and the costs more staggering, than in our all-out economic war with China. China, the American public believes, deserves these tariffs because it is a trading cheater.

Since 2018, the United States has layered tariff upon tariff on Chinese goods. What started as targeted 25 percent duties under Section 301 (tariffs enacted by the president against perceived unfair trade practices) has metastasized into a comprehensive regime. By 2025, the average US tariff on Chinese imports reached 57.6 percent—up from just 3.1 percent in 2017.[209] At the peak in April 2025, before a temporary reduction, US tariffs on China hit 127 percent.[210]

We've gone from essentially free trade to prohibitive tariffs in fewer than eight years. We've added 10 percent "fentanyl" tariffs, 20 percent "reciprocal" tariffs, 25 percent steel and aluminum tariffs, 25 percent auto tariffs, and 50 percent tariffs on various derivatives. We've stacked duty upon duty until our trade policy resembles a very wobbly Jenga tower.

The policy is at fever pitch. It's no longer about specific unfair practices. It's comprehensive economic warfare. And what has it accomplished?

China's industrial base is still kicking. In 2024, China's manufacturing GDP reached $4.67 trillion, up 6 percent year over year.[211] China's industrial output grew 5.2 percent in August 2025 despite the tariffs. Industrial profits in China rose 20.4 percent in August 2025 compared to the prior year, the sharpest rebound in nearly two years.[212] China still accounts for approximately 30 percent of global manufacturing value added, a share that has barely budged despite years of US tariffs.[213]

The Made in China 2025 initiative, which US policymakers tried to strangle with tariffs, has largely achieved its goals of moving into high-tech sectors and reducing dependency on foreign inputs. An April 2025 European Chamber of Commerce report found that China has achieved technological dominance in automotives, shipbuilding, high-speed rail, and EVs, all while operating under the most severe tariff regime in a century.[214]

It is possible our tariffs made China … better? And even more efficient?

Oops. How did that happen?

Tariffs may have slowed the Chinese economy marginally. But marginally slowing a competitor while imposing massive costs on your own economy is not a great strategy.

THE UNINTENDED GIFT TO CHINA

Here's the part that should really haunt American policymakers: Not only did tariffs make China more competitive, but we helped expand its market out of the United States by simultaneously tariffing all our allies. We've accomplished something Beijing could never have achieved on its own: We've pushed our allies into China's arms.

European Union imports from China reached $560 billion in 2024. The EU's trade deficit with China hit €305 billion, the second highest on record.[215] And while US tariffs were ostensibly designed to protect American industry, European companies exporting to the US have been among the beneficiaries of Chinese manufacturing.

More striking: Europe isn't diversifying away from China the way America claims to be. Between 2017 and 2024, the US reduced China's share of its imports by 8.4 percentage points, shifting supply to Vietnam, Mexico, and other countries.[216] But Europe actually deepened its reliance on China during the same period. China's share of EU imports in critical sectors such as electronics, machinery, and clean energy technology has risen.[217]

Why? Because European companies, watching the US–China trade war, didn't want to be caught in the crossfire. So, they secured long-term contracts with Chinese suppliers, built deeper relationships, and integrated Chinese technology into their supply chains.[218] When Trump slapped 25 percent tariffs on European steel and aluminum and threatened 25 percent auto tariffs, European executives concluded that relying on stable Chinese supply chains was less risky than depending on an unpredictable (some might say batshit crazy) American trade policy.

This is the height of strategic incompetence. We meant to isolate China. Instead, we isolated ourselves. We wanted to force allies to choose between the US and China. Instead, we made China look like the more reliable partner.

China's share of exports to the US has fallen from nearly 20 percent in 2017 to under 15 percent today.[219] But total Chinese exports are higher than ever, because China simply redirected its production to markets we abandoned. Chinese companies now export record amounts to Europe, Southeast Asia, Latin America, and Africa. In some categories, Chinese goods still flow into American stores via third countries—bounced through Vietnam or Mexico—so companies can avoid the tariffs. (Yes, there are a bunch of lawyers working on those schemes as well.)

THE COSTS OF TARIFFS ARE BECOMING IMPOSSIBLE TO IGNORE

US tariffs will amount to an average tax increase of $1,300 per household in 2025.[220] That's money pulled out of family budgets—not from some abstract "China," but from Americans buying goods at Target and Walmart. Core goods inflation has risen 1.2 percent year over year through the first quarter of 2025, with economists estimating that tariffs have added 0.3 to 0.8 percentage points to inflation depending on the sector.[221]

The Budget Lab at Yale estimates that all 2025 tariffs will reduce US GDP by 0.9 percentage points in the first year, with persistent effects reducing long-run GDP by $160 billion annually.[222] J.P. Morgan forecasts Personal Consumption Expenditures (PCE) inflation climbing to 2.7 percent in 2025—up from pre-tariff projections—with core inflation hitting 3.1 percent.[223] The Federal Reserve, which had planned multiple interest rate cuts, has effectively gone on hold because tariff-driven inflation has derailed its plans.[224]

Consumer prices for furniture and household equipment have risen 3 percent above 2024 averages, higher than in any other major economy.[225] The Budget Lab at Yale reveals that motor vehicle prices are up 8.4 percent because of auto tariffs, apparel prices have surged 17 percent from all 2025 tariff actions combined, and food prices have increased 2.8 percent, with fresh produce prices up 4 percent.[226]

The Congressional Budget Office estimates that tariffs will increase the average annual inflation rate by roughly 0.4 percentage points over 2025 and 2026.[227] That might sound small, but it's a massive policy own goal: We're making our own citizens poorer to wage economic war on a country that's still growing faster than ours.

We have deployed the most comprehensive tariff regime in a century. We have spent trillions on forgone economic growth. We have raised prices for American consumers. We have alienated our allies. And we have utterly failed to achieve our stated objective, which is to contain China's industrial rise.

It's hard to imagine a more ineffective policy response.

There is a better way.

BRING
JOBS
HOME
NO
MORE
CHINA
TRADE

CHAPTER 8

WHAT THE UNITED STATES SHOULD DO ABOUT CHINA

Tariffs have failed.

But most of the country still believes China is a civilizational rival. If tariffs aren't going to work, what next? Bombs?

The framing around China being a civilizational rival is a trap, and there are scores of examples of countries managing relative shifts in power without digging out the nuclear codes.

A DIFFERENT PARADIGM

There is absolutely another way to see this moment.

How about how Britain handled America's rise in the nineteenth century? By 1890, the United States had become the world's largest economy. American steel undercut British producers, US agriculture flooded European markets, and American manufacturing challenged British dominance.[228] Many in Britain saw this as an existential threat. Yet, instead of trying to contain America, Britain gradually accommodated its rise, ultimately becoming our closest ally. The key was recognizing that interests could align even as relative power shifted.

How about Japan in the 1980s? Japanese manufacturing success triggered panic in Washington. Politicians smashed Toshiba radios on the Capitol steps, convinced Japan's rise meant America's decline. Japanese firms bought Rockefeller Center, Columbia Pictures, and Pebble Beach Golf Links, fueling fears of a national sellout.[229]

Yet, rather than full-scale decoupling, we negotiated agreements such as the Plaza Accord, pressured Japan to open its markets, and invested in our own competitiveness. The result was not a trade war, but a mature partnership between two complementary economies: the kind of relationship that, today, allows companies such as Mr. Tanaka's precision parts firm to thrive as trusted suppliers to American manufacturers.

Even the Cold War offers lessons. For four decades, the US and Soviet Union managed intense rivalry without direct conflict, despite far deeper ideological differences than we have with China. They achieved this through deterrence, clear communication, and limited cooperation on shared interests, such as nuclear safety and space exploration. When both sides understood the rules, competition stayed fierce but controlled.

The Cold War also shows the cost of total separation. After all, the world did split into rigid blocs. As a result, collaboration slowed, and proxy wars devastated smaller nations. Economist David Autor estimates this Cold War technological isolation reduced global innovation by 15 to 20 percent in key sectors.[230] A new Cold War with China—given today's deep economic integration—would be far more destructive, undermining prosperity and weakening America's influence.

History shows that managed rivalry is possible; politics decides whether we try.

China doesn't have to be our twin to be our partner. It can be a separate pillar, different in form but connected in function. Imagine the global economy as an engine with two pistons. One piston is the United States and its allies: chaotic, inventive, endlessly improvising. This is the side that invents airplanes, microchips, and apps no one knew they needed until they couldn't live without them. The other piston is China: vast, coordinated, able to take those sparks of innovation and scale them to world-changing degrees.

These impulses aren't opposites; they can be complementary. We create; they amplify. We improvise; they organize. Consider solar energy: American scientists pioneered solar cells in the 1950s, but Chinese factories made them affordable at scale, dropping global prices by 85 percent between 2010 and 2020.[231] Neither side could have achieved this transformation alone.

The tragedy is that instead of harnessing this potential synergy, we're tearing the engine apart. Tariffs and embargoes slow our own growth and weaken our ability to solve shared challenges such as climate change. US–China trade reached $690 billion in 2022,[232] supporting millions of American jobs and supplying vital revenue for companies such as Apple, Tesla, and Boeing. Breaking these connections fragments the very networks that have driven global prosperity for decades.

Our aim should be to work with China as it is, negotiating where we can, defending where we must, and building rules that make mutual benefit possible. If we can make that shift, trade stops being a weapon and becomes a bridge. Tariffs give way to agreements. Embargoes give way to standards. And rivalry gives way—slowly, imperfectly—to a managed coexistence that benefits us both.

The goal should be what historians call competitive coexistence—a sustained rivalry managed through rules and institutions that prevent it from tipping into war or total disengagement. We've done it before, with Britain, Japan, and even the Soviet Union. We can do it again if we define clear principles for when to compete, when to cooperate, and when to simply coexist.

THE THREE SPHERES OF ENGAGEMENT

This strategic approach requires dividing our relationship with China into three distinct spheres, each with its own logic and tools. Think of it as managing that twin engine: The first sphere builds a protective enclosure to keep our part of the engine safe while it runs, the second creates connection rods that let individually powerful pistons engage the same crankshaft, and the third provides the oil—predictable rules and steady trade—that keeps everything running smoothly. Success depends on keeping these spheres separate while ensuring they reinforce rather than undermine each other.

Of course, these spheres are not hermetically sealed. The most difficult policy challenges will arise at their boundaries, where a single technology or trade issue has implications for all three spheres. Artificial intelligence can simultaneously enable autonomous weapons (competition), accelerate medical research breakthroughs (cooperation), and power everyday consumer applications (coexistence). This is where strategic discipline will be most essential: resisting the temptation to treat every challenge as purely competitive while remaining vigilant about genuine security threats.

SPHERE ONE: COMPETE WHERE WE MUST

Some parts of our relationship with China will always be fundamentally competitive. When Beijing's actions threaten core American interests—our security, our allies, or our fundamental values—we must compete, and we must win. But competition should be strategic, not reflexive.

Technology represents the sharpest edge of this rivalry. Yet, our current approach often resembles using a sledgehammer for surgery. Bloomberg Economics estimates that full technological decoupling could cut global GDP by $3.5 trillion over the next decade.[233] Meanwhile, US companies are already hurting from the disengagement underway. Semiconductor giants such as Qualcomm and Intel have seen China-related revenues fall by 23 percent and 27 percent, respectively, since 2021, forcing cuts to R&D spending precisely when workers need those high-tech manufacturing jobs to stay competitive.[234]

The solution is what experts call a "small yard with a high fence." That means defining a narrow circle of truly sensitive technologies, guarding it fiercely, and leaving everything else open to trade and collaboration. This protects the next generation of innovators without kneecapping the firms that create high-paying jobs.

Inside the high-fenced yard: I am not an expert in this area, but the technologies in the yard are those with direct military or intelligence applications. Advanced semiconductors below fourteen nanometers—the cutting edge of chip manufacturing that enables AI training, missile guidance systems, and advanced surveillance—certainly belong inside the fence because they represent a generational leap in computational power that can be directly weaponized. Also inside: quantum computing hardware that could break encryption, frontier AI training systems capable of autonomous weapons development, hypersonic and directed-energy weapons, and next-gen telecommunications with dual-use potential whereby the same 5G equipment can power civilian networks or military command-and-control systems.

Outside the yard: Beyond the fence are commercially important but nonsensitive technologies. Consumer electronics, renewable energy components, basic manufacturing equipment, educational exchanges in nonsensitive fields, and most commercial space technology should remain open for trade. The twenty-eight-nanometer chips that power most everyday devices—from washing machines to cars—pose no security threat, and blocking them only raises costs for American consumers while pushing China to develop its own alternatives faster.

This strategy requires constant recalibration as today's breakthrough becomes tomorrow's commodity. GPS was once military only; now it's in every smartphone. That means regular reviews by technical experts who understand both the technology and the threat are needed. And it must be multilateral. If the US bans sales while Europe or South Korea do not, China will simply go around us. Building coalitions means compromise; other nations won't copy our list exactly, but they will support shared principles if we treat them as partners rather than subordinates.

SPHERE TWO: COOPERATE ON THE EARTH-SIZED PROBLEMS

While we must compete with China where our core interests are threatened, we should also cooperate wherever interests align, especially on challenges too big for either country to solve alone. This is where the twin engine metaphor becomes practical policy: America drives innovation, China brings scaling power, and together they move the world forward.

Climate change represents an essential partnership. Data from 2022 estimate that China emits roughly 30% of global CO_2, and the United States around 14%, meaning the two together account for nearly 44% of global emissions.[235] Without those countries' cooperation, limiting warming to 1.5°C is virtually impossible. History shows that this cooperation is possible. The 2021 Glasgow Climate Pact emerged from quiet negotiations led by John Kerry and Xie Zhenhua[236]—proof that even in a bad season, deals are possible.

We should build on that success by creating Climate Action Innovation Zones: designated areas in which US and Chinese companies collaborate under strict rules. Advanced battery storage could pair US research with Chinese manufacturing to deliver grid-scale storage for renewable energy. Carbon capture and storage could combine American innovation with Chinese engineering for large-scale deployment. Green hydrogen could merge US fuel cell breakthroughs with Chinese scale to drive costs low enough to compete with fossil fuels.

These partnerships would include clear IP protections, measurable targets, and transparent rules. Recent history shows what's at stake: Wind turbine costs dropped 70 percent between 2010 and 2020 thanks to Chinese scaling of Western technology.[237] Expanding this model could accelerate bilateral global fixes to big problems while creating new markets for both nations. Medical coordination, AI research, space debris cleanup, ocean research, water resource management—all areas desperate for truly global cooperation.

These institutions would involve multiple countries, with shared oversight and strict rules to keep sensitive military research off the table. For cooperation to last, it must be structured to withstand political storms. Even during the Cold War, US–Soviet scientific collaboration endured because it was institutionalized and clearly defined. Durable cooperation is project focused, transparent, multilateral, reciprocal, and built with escape hatches.

The International Space Station proves this model works. Even after Russia's invasion of Ukraine, astronauts from both countries continued working together in orbit because the partnership served shared, well-defined interests. By applying these same principles to US–China cooperation, we can keep the twin engines running even when politics heats up on the ground.

SPHERE THREE: COEXIST AND PROSPER EVERYWHERE ELSE

For more than 95 percent of the goods and services involved in the US–China economic relationship, it simply doesn't matter who makes what. Phones, apparel, furniture, basic electronics, midrange auto parts: These aren't national secrets; they're global commodities. Here, the strategy should be boring and bold: Let free trade work. Comparative advantage will sort production efficiently; consumers will get lower prices; firms will keep innovating. Our job is to provide a predictable, rules-based floor and then get out of the way.

What actually needs adjusting isn't the flow of goods so much as the flow of capital. Trade deficits reflect deeper savings–investment patterns, not moral failure. If we want a "fairer" deficit, the most constructive lever is opening the Chinese capital account so that Chinese savings can also flow into US assets, not just into state-owned companies and trade surpluses. That means pushing China to let the Ms. Chens have the freedom to invest where they may. That means pushing China to gradually liberalize outbound investment channels, widening household investment options and allowing more currency flexibility—steps that naturally ease persistent imbalances without taxing American families at the checkout line.

Regarding supply chains, the pandemic taught us about single-point supply fragility. In other words, it's dangerous to have China make everything. But that in no way means that everything must move home. Full reshoring would cost $1 trillion to $2 trillion and lift consumer prices 15 to 25 percent—a cure worse than the disease.[238] The smarter play is regional diversification. For critical goods, diversify sources across trusted partners; for important systems, demand transparency so investors can price resilience; and for the vast middle of everyday trade, let markets run under basic labor and safety rules. Resilience is a portfolio, not a postcode.

When Beijing weaponizes trade—leveraging boycotts against Australia, placing pressure on Lithuania—the answer isn't decoupling from the world's second-largest economy; it's collective action. Think an economic NATO with our allies: calibrated trade countermeasures that raise the cost of Chinese coercion, should it arise.

Bottom line: For the overwhelming majority of commerce, comparative advantage should rule. Open capital channels, nudge firms toward regional diversity (already underway), keep targeted guardrails where truly necessary—and otherwise, step aside and let prosperity compound.

BUILDING THE INFRASTRUCTURE FOR PEACE

Competition without communication is dangerous. During the Cold War, the US and Soviet Union maintained hotlines and arms-control talks even at the height of rivalry. Today, the US and China lack even basic crisis channels. Recent incidents show the risk: In 2023, a Chinese surveillance balloon drifted over the US with almost no direct military communication. In 2022, Chinese aircraft intercepted US reconnaissance flights with no clear protocols to prevent escalation.

We need essential guardrails: military hotlines between operational commanders; regular leader summits to keep dialogue open during crises; working-level dialogues among diplomats, economists, and technical experts; and crisis protocols for maritime or aerial incidents. Predictability prevents accidents from becoming wars. Talk early, talk often, talk when it's hardest.

This infrastructure must extend beyond government. Academic exchanges, business dialogues, and cultural programs create constituencies for stability in both countries. When Shanghai businessmen and Iowa farmers share interests in trade, politicians find it harder to burn bridges completely.

And then there's Taiwan, the single issue that could turn managed competition into open conflict overnight. Given my history, I am deeply sympathetic to the plight of Taiwan, but I'll save a full treatment of that island for another book. I'll only say one thing: The greatest threat to Taiwan isn't China's aggression alone; it's the unraveling of economic engagement between the US and China.

Taiwan's democracy and safety are strongest when everyone has more to lose than to gain from conflict. For forty years, that has been the quiet genius of the status quo. China prospers through peaceful trade. The United States sustains its influence through open markets and deterrence. Taiwan thrives in the middle: prosperous, self-governing, and indispensable to the global economy. That balance holds not because everyone is perfectly happy with it, but because everyone understands the alternative would be ruinous.

Strategic ambiguity—Washington's deliberate refusal to say exactly how it would respond to an invasion—works only when both sides value stability more than confrontation. If Beijing starts believing it has already lost America as a trading partner, while Washington grows hesitant or inconsistent in its commitments, that equilibrium begins to crack. If fear replaces profit as the dominant logic in China, then the probability of a Chinese miscalculation rises.

Taiwan's peace depends not just on military deterrence but on economic interdependence running at full strength.

BUILDING SUPPORT FOR NUANCE

This strategy will fail without domestic support, which requires showing Americans that smart engagement protects their concrete interests. And I'll be blunt: Yes, as an outsourcer, I profit from trade with China. But so do farmers in Iowa, machinists in Ohio, and engineers in Arizona—often on the same project.

Advocating for deeper engagement with China today is politically dangerous. According to Pew Research's 2023 survey, a substantial majority of Americans view China unfavorably—the highest share in decades—and unfavorable sentiment is especially pronounced among Republicans.[239] Any leader who argues for nuance risks being branded soft on an authoritarian rival—a stooge for the Evil Empire.

Yet public opinion is more sophisticated than the headlines suggest. When asked about specific issues, support varies widely. Seventy-three percent of Americans support limiting Chinese investment in sensitive technologies, but only 45 percent favor broad trade restrictions that would raise prices. Meanwhile, 67 percent support cooperation on climate change, and 71 percent support cooperation on pandemic preparedness, even as they oppose military aggression and influence operations.[240] This shows space for a sophisticated strategy that competes where necessary while cooperating where possible.

Crucially, public opinion follows leadership. Franklin Roosevelt didn't wait for the American public to demand aid to Britain in World War II—he built the case for it. Today's leaders must do the same: explain why smart competition with China protects American interests better than destructive isolation. The argument is pragmatic. Total decoupling would destroy American jobs, slow innovation, and leave global crises unsolved while alienating allies who refuse to choose sides in our manufactured conflict.

The constituencies are there, and they have faces: US agriculture depends on China buying $24 billion in US farm goods annually, supporting over two hundred thousand jobs in swing states—jobs that keep communities such as Lisa's alive.[241] Technology firms earned $55 billion in Chinese revenue in 2022, and Apple alone employs 250,000 people through its China supply chain.[242] Manufacturing companies such as Boeing estimate that losing Chinese suppliers would raise aircraft costs by 15 to 20 percent and delay deliveries by up to a year.[243]

The key is showing that smart engagement protects these industries while addressing legitimate security concerns. A soybean farmer, such as Lisa, and a software engineer may vote differently, but both benefit from stability. Small business owners, such as Mike, need predictable rules to plan their exports, while workers, such as Darrell, need the high-tech manufacturing jobs that come from integrated supply chains. Even our allies, such as Mr. Tanaka and his company in Japan, depend on stable US–China relations to avoid being forced to choose sides.

America stands at a crossroads. We can continue on the current path, viewing every interaction with China through the lens of civilizational conflict, walling off our economies, and forcing the world to choose sides. Or we can choose strategic clarity: compete where we must to protect our security and vital technologies, cooperate where we can on global challenges such as climate change and pandemics, and coexist everywhere else through stable, rules-based trade that lifts both nations.

Some say this is naïve softness. I think that it's strength, informed by history and cultural understanding. It's the confidence to compete fiercely, the vision to cooperate where the world needs us, and the maturity to coexist with a country that will never look exactly like ours.

This choice will determine whether Lisa's farm thrives or shuts down under retaliatory tariffs, whether Mike's small business can compete globally or gets trapped in a fragmented market, whether

Darrell's children inherit high-tech manufacturing jobs or see them disappear behind trade walls, and whether allies such as Mr. Tanaka's company stand with us or, out of frustration, choose the other side.

The world needs as many engines of growth as we can muster.

Let's repair the one we started ripping apart.

BRING JOBS HOME
NO MORE CHINA TRADE

CHAPTER 9

WHAT YOU CAN DO ABOUT CHINA

Policy is written in capital cities.

Power is not.

Real power lives elsewhere: In the millions of quiet, transactional, human connections that link factories and classrooms, investors and inventors, buyers and dreamers. It lives in emails, purchase orders, student visas, joint research papers, and awkward first dinners where nobody quite understands the menu.

Our task, then, is not to wait for a redesigned world order from Washington or Beijing. That will take longer than any of us has patience for. Our task is to double down on where the United States and China already meet. Not in press releases or summits, but through people like you and me, and through China's pragmatic, commercially minded periphery.

If there are a few hundred official communiqués exchanged between our governments each year, it is no exaggeration to say there are millions between businesses, universities, families, and individuals. That is where the relationship actually exists. That is where it is negotiated, repaired, tested, and—more often than not—kept alive.

We should start by acknowledging that reality.

We can trade even while our political centers struggle to define the future and to understand each other's intentions. That struggle will continue for decades. But trade does not need to wait for philosophical clarity. It never has.

As this book has argued, the divide between China and the West is deeper than democracy versus authoritarianism, capitalism versus socialism, or individual rights versus collective good. It is a disagreement about how societies face uncertainty itself. When the future becomes uncertain, China's instinct is to narrow the range of possible outcomes, to guide society toward safety through control and coordination. The American instinct is typically to widen the field, accepting volatility in the belief that open markets and free actors will discover a solution no planner can foresee.

And here, despite my deep affection for China, my bet remains with the American tradition.

America built its prosperity on what Adam Smith called the invisible hand: the idea that when individuals pursue their own interests within a stable framework of rules, collective progress emerges without central design. Prices are discovered. Opportunities are found. Innovation arises not from foresight, but from experimentation. The system works precisely because no one claims to know the future.

China rejects this premise. As economist Lan Xiaohuan writes, "China does not believe in the invisible hand because the goals of the hand are invisible." That sentence captures the civilizational divide better than any policy paper ever could.

To China's leaders, a society that does not know where it is going is a society that has lost its way. The purpose of government is not merely to referee, but to guide: to act as a visible hand that steers the nation toward prosperity, stability, and dignity. This impulse is not politically cynical. It is moral. It stretches back centuries to the Mandate of Heaven and forward to Xi Jinping's insistence on common prosperity.

I understand that impulse deeply. I am even tempted by it.

But I do not believe it works. At least not in the long run.

THE PERIPHERY'S RECURRING RESCUE

Here's the familiar pattern that has repeated itself throughout Chinese history: The ruling moral center grows larger, then more rigid, then ossifies; the periphery improvises, reality forces adaptation, and the center claims credit for reforms it initially opposed.

Ray Huang's masterwork, *1587, A Year of No Significance*, describes a Ming Dynasty court trapped in moral performance, and that is "too strong to change."[244] Confucian bureaucrats spent their energy writing memorials about ritual propriety while the empire slowly lost vitality. Yet, beyond their view, in the villages and market towns, people were quietly figuring out how to survive: smuggling grain when state monopolies created famines, building protocapitalist trading networks when official edicts restricted commerce.

Here's the familiar pattern that has repeated itself throughout Chinese history: The ruling moral center grows larger, then more rigid, then ossifies; the periphery improvises, reality forces adaptation, and the center claims credit for reforms it initially opposed.

This is the periphery's power. And it inevitably rises again and again.

In the late 1970s and 1980s, it was not Beijing that revived the Chinese economy. It was farmers, emerging from a decade of hunger, responding to food scarcity through what came to be called the Household Responsibility System. In practice, it meant little more than allowing families to work their own plots for their own benefit, rather than being told what to grow and when.

The same logic soon spread beyond the fields. Township and Village Enterprises—nominally collective but functionally private—ignited rural industrialization by applying farmer incentives to small factories. Local officials, desperate for tax revenue and employment, tolerated these market experiments long before the center formally embraced them. The special economic zones where free enterprise was permitted to take root, places like Shenzhen, were tightly controlled exceptions, designed to fail quietly or succeed usefully. When they succeeded, Beijing retroactively canonized them.

Even China's modern private sector—now employing more than 80 percent of urban workers—was born in legal gray zones where property rights were unclear and entrepreneurship was technically illegal. Reform did not arrive through the front door; it came in from a warehouse window.

The same story played out in the Digital Age. Alibaba, Tencent, and ByteDance were not designed by industrial planners. They emerged faster than regulators could understand them. Jack Ma's famous line—better to ask forgiveness than permission—was an actual business model. For years, China's most dynamic firms lived in the space between tolerance and neglect.[245]

The center claims credit for these successes now, but it was the periphery that made them possible.

Holding the respect and admiration of China's periphery should be America's most ardent foreign policy objective.

You and I are more responsible for that than the State Department.

TWO PROGNOSES: LARDY'S ALARM AND LAN'S CONFIDENCE

In the debate about China's future, it's hard to know where the Middle Kingdom will land. Is China entering a period of managed decline—slow, rigid, self-inflicted—or executing a deliberate transition toward a new, coordinated model of capitalism that the West simply doesn't understand?

Two great thinkers personify opposing views.

Nicholas Lardy, a senior fellow at the Peterson Institute, has spent decades studying China's economy with the kind of granular attention that comes from actually reading Chinese financial reports. His 2019 book, *The State Strikes Back*, documents what he describes as a disturbing reversal: After three decades of liberalization, China's state is reasserting control over the economy.

The numbers tell his story. In 2013, when Xi Jinping came to power, state-owned enterprises accounted for about 30 percent of industrial profits while employing 20 percent of workers. By 2019, their share of profits had shrunk even as their access to credit expanded dramatically. Meanwhile, private firms—which generate the vast majority of China's innovation, exports, and employment—saw their access to bank loans decline. Credit was being diverted from productive private firms to politically favored state giants "for reasons of policy, not productivity."[246]

The result, Lardy argues, is predictable: falling productivity growth, declining private investment, and a slowdown that is entirely self-inflicted. Ideology has replaced economics. The invisible hand that unleashed China's dynamism is being tied behind the state's back.

Lan Xiaohuan, an economist from China Europe International Business School, whom I quoted above, sees the same data differently. To him, the resurgence of the state is not regression but evolution, a "meta-market" model whereby the Party coordinates competition and corrects capitalism's moral blind spots.[247] Where Lardy sees distortion, Lan sees design. The visible hand is not crushing the market; it's guiding it toward socially beneficial outcomes that pure markets would never produce on their own.

Lan points to China's infrastructure achievements. He points to poverty alleviation: eight hundred million people lifted out of extreme poverty since 1980, with the final one hundred million cases achieved between 2012 and 2020 through targeted state campaigns.[248] He argues that China's state acts as an entrepreneurial coordinator, making long-term investments that private capital won't touch and ensuring that growth serves national goals rather than just shareholder returns.

Both men are brilliant. Both marshal impressive evidence. And both are revealing something true about China's predicament.

Lardy is right that the numbers don't lie: When states allocate capital for political rather than economic reasons, productivity suffers. Between 2007 and 2018, total factor productivity growth in China's state sector was essentially zero, while private sector productivity grew by nearly 3 percent annually.[249] That's the difference between stagnation and dynamism, and it shows up in every economy that has tried to replace markets with planning.

But Lan is also right that markets alone don't build nations. Big goals such as infrastructure and poverty-alleviation campaigns require coordination at scales that markets struggle to achieve. Sometimes the visible hand does see more than the invisible one—at least in the short run. America's infrastructure weakness and its rich–poor divide are offered as evidence of what happens when the invisible hand lacks a body moving with purpose.

The harder question for Lan, and for China, is what happens when the state's promise of certainty collides with the reality of rapid economic and social change.

THE INVISIBLE FUTURE

What happens when the trillions China has invested in solar manufacturing meet a breakthrough in fusion energy? When forty-five thousand kilometers of high-speed rail face a future of autonomous flight, virtual presence, or demographic collapse? What happens when today's moral imperative—carbon neutrality, industrial self-sufficiency, national industrial champions—runs headlong into a technological shift that no committee anticipated?

Central planning cannot answer these questions because it assumes the questions are answerable. It requires knowing where we're going so it can guide us there. The invisible hand accepts that the future is fundamentally unknowable and builds institutions designed to adapt rather than predict.

The difference is theological and a matter of faith. The visible hand believes it can foresee the good; the invisible hand believes good emerges from discovery. One worships virtue; the other, variation. One demands that someone be in charge; the other asserts that no one has to be.

That's why America, for all its dysfunction, still produces more transformative innovation than any empire in history. Our strength is not foresight but tolerance for error—even political error. The invisible hand works because it's allowed to fail in public.

Google can launch and abandon dozens of products without threatening social stability. American entrepreneurs can fail seven times before succeeding on the eighth without being accused of moral corruption. An election cycle can wash away political ineptitude when people lose patience. Our system is messy, wasteful, and often deeply unfair—but it's also adaptive and restorative.

China's challenge demands an ability to work out answers to nearly impossible questions: Can a system built on moral certainty coexist with a world prone to probabilistic change? Can the visible hand guide an economy when it cannot see where the economy is going just beyond the horizon?

Personally, I doubt it. At least not in the long run.

But I will let China prove me wrong.

AMERICA'S DANGEROUS IMITATION

That's why our response to China bothers me: It's a response that has made us more like China.

Faced with the challenge of China's state-directed capitalism, we've abandoned our own principles. We've replaced free trade with half-baked industrial policy. We've substituted targeted tariffs with blanket protectionism. We've turned technology competition into ideological warfare. In short, we've tried to beat China by adopting its playbook: using centralization, moral certainty, and an increasingly visible hand.

Here is an alphabet soup of existing US subsidies: The CHIPS and Science Act (2022), the Inflation Reduction Act (2022), the Infrastructure Investment and Jobs Act (2021), the Farm Bill (2018), the Advanced Technology Vehicles Manufacturing Loan Program (2007), and the creative reuse of the Defense Production Act (1950/2018), just to name a few.

Some may be needed. Some may be providing the nation with more security.

But I doubt it.

For sure, they are not creating more jobs.

What worries me most is that underneath the strategic rhetoric about countering China lies a deeper capitulation: the belief that free markets cannot compete with state planning, that the invisible hand needs to be replaced with a more visible one, that maybe China is right after all.

But this is precisely wrong.

We win not by imitating China's centralization but by being more fully ourselves. Our competitive advantage has never been better planning—we've always been bad at that. It's been better adaptation. We don't win by predicting which technologies will matter in 2040; we win by creating the conditions whereby thousands of entrepreneurs can place thousands of different bets, most of which fail, but some of which change the world.

We win not by imitating China's centralization but by being more fully ourselves.

Consider some of the most transformative American companies of the past three decades: Amazon, Google, Meta, Microsoft, Moderna, NVIDIA. Not one was the product of industrial policy. Not one emerged from a state-coordinated plan to dominate a strategic sector. They were all wild bets made by people pursuing visions that most experts considered unlikely or impossible. They succeeded not because government picked them, but because government let them try.

When we abandon that model, we lose. When we start moralizing investment, casting market outcomes as virtues or vices, or demanding certainty where uncertainty is unavoidable, we trade our adaptive advantage for the illusion of control.

Then we may as well surrender now.

There is a deep irony here: In trying to out-plan China, we abandon the one system China has never been able to replicate: an economy that survives being wrong.

WHAT WE CAN DO POLITICALLY

Instead of American central planning, or waging trade wars, we should:

SUPPORT THE PERIPHERY

The Chinese economic periphery is the most potent economic force on planet Earth. They operate not only in China, but in SE Asia, Africa, New York City, and, um, well, everywhere else human beings live. Learn to discern what is the Chinese state, and what is genuine private business. Almost anything you have touched in the last year, from your takeout dinner to your Amazon package, is private. Keep buying. You will change the course of Chinese history as these dynamos breathe vitality back into the Chinese moral system. Maintain ties with China's municipal governments, universities, and civil society organizations. These are the nodes through which reform has historically entered the system.

ABANDON TARIFFS

Trade is not a concession we grant China; it's an investment in China's pragmatic future, in its people, and most critically in our own prosperity. Every commercial relationship between an American buyer and a Chinese supplier is a mini non-aggression pact.

> **Every commercial relationship between an American buyer and a Chinese supplier is a mini non-aggression pact.**

ENCOURAGE EDUCATIONAL EXCHANGE

In the 2022–23 academic year, Chinese students represented 27 percent of all international students in the United States—about 290,000 individuals.[250] But they are starting to go elsewhere because they feel less and less welcome. That is a national disgrace and a national mistake. These students not only aid American research and help American companies when they graduate, they return to China having experienced American openness firsthand. They've seen how messy our democracy can be, yes, but also how free markets generate prosperity and how pluralism produces innovation. Not all become advocates for Western values, but all become harder for Beijing to propagandize.

RESPECT THE REFLEX

We must recognize that moral centralism will always re-emerge in Beijing. It's not an ideological quirk of communism; it's a civilizational reflex. Every time China liberalizes, it eventually recentralizes to relegitimize. This has been the pattern for centuries, and it will continue. The goal isn't to eradicate that reflex—we cannot. The goal is to mitigate its costs by keeping engagement alive so reality continues to whisper through the walls of China's moral ideology.

LEAD WITH CONFIDENCE

The United States wins by being the world's most attractive ecosystem, not its most strident lecturer and tariff bully. That means doubling down on what made us successful: open research universities, immigration that attracts global talent, alliances built on mutual benefit rather than coercion, and markets that allow the best ideas to win regardless of where they originate.

The invisible hand is intriguingly welcoming precisely because it doesn't clench into a fist. Between 1990 and 2020, more than 2.3 million Chinese citizens became permanent US residents.[251] They came here not because they were forced but because they saw something in our system they couldn't find at home: the freedom to pursue their own vision of success without asking permission from any moral authority—however enlightened that authority may be.

SEPARATE COMPETITION FROM CATASTROPHE

There are genuine areas in which American and Chinese interests conflict. We should compete vigorously in those domains. But competition should sharpen us. (Just as competition with Japan sharpened us.) What we shouldn't do is treat every Chinese success as an American failure, every Chinese company as a security threat, every Chinese student as a potential spy.

KEEP INVESTING

Resist the moral panic of total divestment. Evaluate Chinese companies—and American companies with exposure to China—on their fundamentals, not their flags. The Chinese economy produces real value; don't let political theater blind you to it.

KEEP BUYING

Continue to buy from China when it makes sense. That small business, such as my sister's, importing goods from a Chinese supplier, isn't funding the Party's ambitions; it's sustaining a pragmatic people-to-people network that keeps both economies vibrantly alive. Value matters more than origin.

KEEP LEARNING

China is not going away. Choose to study Chinese language, history, or business rather than treating an entire civilization as off-limits. The better Americans understand China's complexity, the harder it becomes for politicians to weaponize ignorance.

KEEP WELCOMING

Welcome the Chinese family who moves in down the street, the Chinese colleague who joins your team, the Chinese graduate student studying at your local university. Every human connection is a chance to make your own narrative about China, rather than absorbing it through a marinade of unresearched rumor and innuendo.

AND, FINALLY, VOTE BETTER

Demand nuance from your representatives. Ask them not just what they'll do about China but how they'll distinguish merely commercial competition from genuine security risk; how they'll support American workers without propping up inefficient companies for the next 240 years; how they'll encourage the changes we want to see in China without inviting retaliation.

A FAR REACHING CONCLUSION

The invisible hand of trade is nothing more than human hands reaching out for a better life.

And that reach rarely starts as a search for friendship. More often than not it moves forward in hesitation, sometimes in distrust, sometimes even in quiet disdain. We reach out not because we admire the person across the table, or share their politics or creed, but because our trade requires it. Trade has never been sentimental. It only demands you acknowledge that the other person exists, and that they have something you want.

I have done business with people I would never otherwise have engaged. Communists. Muslims. Party members loyal to systems that reject nearly everything I believe about politics, religion, and freedom. We did not meet to reconcile worldviews. We met to trade. We signed contracts. We shipped goods. We paid invoices. And somewhere along the way, without even trying to, we discovered one another's humanity. Very often, we ended up as friends despite having so little in common on the surface.

My brother, an evangelical Christian, has a business utterly enmeshed with a Jewish family business in New Jersey. Their theology diverges on many essential points, I'm sure. Mine is with a sworn member of the Chinese Communist Party, who was once a soldier for the People's Liberation Army. Sometimes we debate politics. But mostly we just transact.

And that turns out to be enough.

This is not kumbaya. Trade does not ask for agreement, conversion, or affection. It demands cooperation, which is narrow, disciplined, and voluntary. But that discipline carries a radical assumption: that the person across from you is rational, purposeful, and trustworthy enough to keep their word. Once you grant that, the grand labels begin to shrink. Communist. Capitalist. Christian. Muslim. Jew. What remains is something older and sturdier: just two people seeking mutual gain without mutual harm.

Adam Smith understood this intuitively. Exchange, he said, enlarges sympathy through repeated contact. Hayek expanded it: Trade is cooperation without consensus, order without command.

This is why trade matters. And why its collapse is so dangerous.

When trade barriers arise, the trading hand is forced to retract. When the hand retracts, the practice of learned sympathy dies. Nations, and their peoples, harden into abstractions. Politics rushes in to finish the job.

The invisible hand of trade was never a promise of harmony. It was the forced discipline of continuing to make contact no matter what: Forcing people who would otherwise remain strangers, or enemies, to deal with one another honestly, again and again.

The result is the slow manufacture of genuine sympathy. And it is the greatest force for peace the world has ever known. It reminds us, practically, that we are human before we are anything else.

In a world desperate to divide, that reluctant hand reaching out to trade may be the last working instrument keeping us from an apocalyptic oblivion; the last thing reminding us that no one nation (and no one individual) can live alone in a silo. Abundance, both emotional and economic, only happens when two people face each other, dig deep for sympathy, and exchange.

The challenge, then, is not to wait for our governments to trade, but to decide whether you will trade. Whether you will keep your hand extended. Whether you will reach across lines others tell you are impassable.

If I have earned any of your trust with this book, I can tell you it's worth it.

I have lived my entire life this way. In between.

Haphazardly bouncing into strangers. Surprised to end up with a world of friends.

I refuse to live any other way.

BRING
JOBS
HOME
NO
MORE
CHINA
TRADE

BIBLIOGRAPHY

Acheson, Dean. United States Relations with China: With Special Reference to the Period 1944–1949. US Government Printing Office, 1949.

"Amerasia Case Summary." File 65-56402. Federal Bureau of Investigation Records, National Archives and Records Administration, 1945.

American Board of Commissioners for Foreign Missions. *Annual Report of the American Board of Commissioners for Foreign Missions*. Vol. 51. American Board of Commissioners for Foreign Missions, 1860. Yale Divinity Library digital collection.

American Board of Commissioners for Foreign Missions. *Annual Report of the American Board of Commissioners for Foreign Missions*. Vol 41. American Board of Commissioners for Foreign Missions, 1850. Yale Divinity Library digital collection.

Amiti, Mary, and Donald R. Davis. *Trade, Firms, and Wages: Theory and Evidence*. Federal Reserve Bank of New York and Columbia University, 2011. https://www.newyorkfed.org/medialibrary/media/research/economists/amiti/wages_amiti_davis.pdf.

Apple Inc. *SEC Filings: Greater China Revenue, 2021*. Apple Inc., 2021. https://investor.apple.com/sec-filings/sec-filings-details/default.aspx?FilingId=15311311.

Autor, David H. "Trade and Labor Markets: Lessons from China's Rise." *IZA World of Labor.* 2018. https://doi.org/10.15185/izawol.431.

Autor, David H., David Dorn, and Gordon H. Hanson. "The China Shock: Learning from Labor Market Adjustment to Large Changes in Trade." *Annual Review of Economics* 8 (2016): 205–40.

Barbiero, Omar, and Hillary Stein. "The Impact of Tariffs on Inflation." Current Policy Perspectives. *Federal Reserve Bank of Boston.* February 6, 2025. https://www.bostonfed.org/publications/current-policy-perspectives/2025/the-impact-of-tariffs-on-inflation.

Benson, Emily, and Claire Y. Li. "China's New Economic Statecraft: Industrial Subsidies and Strategic Industries." Center for Strategic and International Studies, 2023.

Bertrand, Savannah. "Fact Sheet | Proposals to Reduce Fossil Fuel Subsidies (2021)." *Environmental and Energy Study Institute.* July 23, 2021. https://www.eesi.org/papers/view/fact-sheet-proposals-to-reduce-fossil-fuel-subsidies-2021.

Blackburn, Marsha (@MarshaBlackburn). "China has a 5,000 year history of cheating and stealing. Some things will never change ..." Twitter (now X). December 3, 2020. https://x.com/MarshaBlackburn/status/1334510812552163328.

Bloomberg. "China's Population Shrinks for First Time in Six Decades." *TIME.* January 17, 2023. https://time.com/6247641/china-population-decline-six-decades.

Boeing. "Fast-Growing China Domestic Air Travel Driving 20-Year Demand for 8,560 Airplanes." Press release, September 20, 2023. https://boeing.mediaroom.com/2023-09-19-Boeing-Fast-growing-China-domestic-air-travel-driving-20-year-demand-for-8,560-airplanes.

Bown, Chad P. "US-China Trade War Tariffs: An Up-to-Date Chart." *Peterson Institute for International Economics*. August 27, 2025. https://www.piie.com/research/piie-charts/2019/us-china-trade-war-tariffs-date-chart.

Brailo, Andy, David A. Hargraves, and Matt Bossemeyer. "Premier Data: The State of PPE Supply One Year into COVID-19." *Premier Inc.* April 1, 2021. https://premierinc.com/newsroom/blog/premier-data-the-state-of-ppe-supply-one-year-in-to-covid-19.

British Council. *Annual Report and Accounts 2022–23*. British Council, 2023. https://www.britishcouncil.org/sites/default/files/britishcouncil_annualreport_2022-23.pdf.

Budgetary and Economic Effects of Increases in Tariffs Implemented Between January 6 and May 13, 2025. Congressional Budget Office. 2025. https://www.cbo.gov/publication/61389.

Bush, George W. "Transcript: Bush Describes U.S. Values to Chinese Students." Transcript of remarks at Tsinghua University. February 22, 2002. https://usinfo.org/wf-archive/2002/020222/epf502.htm.

Business Roundtable. "Trade and American Jobs: The Impact of Trade on US and State-Level Employment, 2022 Update." February 28, 2022. https://www.businessroundtable.org/trade-and-american-jobs-the-impact-of-trade-on-us-and-state-level-employment-2022-update.

Centers for Disease Control and Prevention, National Center for Health Statistics. "COVID-19 Mortality." August 20, 2025. https://www.cdc.gov/nchs/state-stats/deaths/covid19.html.

Chang, Gordon. *The Coming Collapse of China*. Random House, 2001.

Chen, Xiangming, and Youquin Huang. "China's Urbanization and Migration: Policy, Population, and Social Consequences." *Cities* 104

(2020): 102770. https://www.sciencedirect.com/science/article/abs/pii/S0166046220303239.

Chicago Council on Global Affairs. *American Public Opinion and US Foreign Policy 2023*. September 2023.

Chimits, François. "Growing Asymmetry: Mapping the Import Dependencies in EU and US Trade with China." *Mercator Institute for China Studies*. October 1, 2024. https://merics.org/en/report/growing-asymmetry-mapping-import-dependencies-eu-and-us-trade-china.

China Association of Automobile Manufacturers. "2023 Auto Sales Data." January 2024. http://www.caam.org.cn/data/2023-auto-sales.

China Association of Automobile Manufacturers. "2024 Vehicle Sales of China." *Asian Automotive Analysis*, April 7, 2025. https://aaa.fourin.com/reports/0216b120-137a-11f0-a1e1-630064034eb7/2024-vehicle-sales-of-china.

ChinaAid. *Annual Report: Religious Persecution Statistics, 2023*. ChinaAid, 2023. https://chinaaid.org/news/stories-by-issue/advocacy/chinaaid-releases-annual-persecution-report-for-2023/.

ChinaFile. "US–China Trade Stayed Robust in 2022. Will That Last?" March 13, 2023. https://www.chinafile.com/conversation/us-china-trade-stayed-robust-2022-will-last.

Clark, Duncan. Alibaba: The House That Jack Ma Built. Ecco, 2016.

Clarke, Toni. "India's Ranbaxy Hit by FDA Product Ban at Fourth Indian Plant." *Reuters*. January 24, 2014. https://www.reuters.com/article/business/indias-ranbaxy-hit-by-fda-product-ban-at-4th-indian-plant-idUSBREA0N070/.

Climate Action Tracker. "Global Update: Paris Agreement Turning Point." December 2021. https://climateactiontracker.org/publications/global-update-paris-agreement-turning-point/.

Clinton, William J. "Full Text of Clinton's Speech on China Trade Bill." Speech at the Paul H. Nitze School of Advanced International Studies, Johns Hopkins University. March 8, 2000. https://www.iatp.org/sites/default/files/Full_Text_of_Clintons_Speech_on_China_Trade_Bi.htm.

Clinton, William J. "Remarks on Permanent Normal Trade Relations with China." In *Public Papers of the Presidents of the United States: William J. Clinton*, bk. 1. US Government Printing Office, 2000. https://www.govinfo.gov/content/pkg/PPP-2000-book1/html/PPP-2000-book1-doc-pg962.htm.

Confucius. *Analects.* Translated by Edward Slingerland. Hackett Publishing, 2003.

Congressional Record. 81st Cong., 2nd sess. February 20, 1950, 96:3452–456.

Coppola, Gabrielle. "Once a Trump Favorite, Harley Now Feels the Pinch of the Trade War." *Bloomberg.* June 25, 2018. https://www.bloomberg.com/news/articles/2018-06-25/harley-davidson-to-shift-motorbike-production-to-counter-tariffs.

"Correctly Viewing the Two Historical Periods Before and After Reform and Opening Up—Studying General Secretary Xi Jinping's Important Discussion on 'Two Things That Cannot Be Negated.'" *People's Daily.* November 8, 2013.

Cotton, Tom. "Seven Things You Can't Say About China." Lecture presented at the Hudson Institute, Washington, DC. February 16, 2025. https://www.hudson.org/events/seven-things-you-cant-say-about-china-senator-tom-cotton-john-walters.

Council on Foreign Relations. "What Happened When China Joined the WTO?" Last updated February 6, 2025. https://education.cfr.org/learn/reading/what-happened-when-china-joined-wto.

Countryeconomy.com. "Taiwan GDP - Gross Domestic Product." https://countryeconomy.com/gdp/taiwan.

Davidson, Jason W. "The Costs of War to United States Allies Since 9/11." *Brown University*. May 12, 2021. https://costsofwar.watson.brown.edu/paper/costs-war-united-states-allies-911.

DiPippo, Gerard, Francesca Ghiretti, and Benjamin Lenain. "Beyond Tariffs: What the US Can Learn From China's Industrial Playbook." *RAND Corporation*. April 17, 2025. https://www.rand.org/pubs/commentary/2025/04/beyond-tariffs-what-the-us-can-learn-from-chinas-industrial.html.

Donnan, Sean, and Enda Curran. "The Global Economy Enters an Era of Upheaval." *Bloomberg*. September 18, 2023. https://www.bloomberg.com/graphics/2023-geopolitical-investments-economic-shift.

Dybisz, Joseph. *Trade Adjustment Assistance*. White paper. Northeast-Midwest Institute, 2019. https://www.nemw.org/wp-content/uploads/2019/09/Trade-Adjustment-Assistance-White-Paper.pdf.

European Commission. *Eurostat Trade Statistics, 2024–2025*. https://ec.europa.eu/eurostat/web/international-trade-in-goods.

European Commission. "REPowerEU: Joint European Action for More Affordable, Secure and Sustainable Energy." Press release. March 8, 2022. https://ec.europa.eu/commission/presscorner/detail/en/ip_22_1511.

Fairbank, John King. *The Missionary Enterprise in China and America*. Harvard University Press, 1974.

Fairbank, John King. *The United States and China*. Harvard University Press, 1979.

Fallows, James. "Containing Japan." *The Atlantic*, May 1989. https://www.theatlantic.com/magazine/archive/1989/05/containing-japan/376337.

FDI Insider. "Significant Decline in Foreign Direct Investment in Asia in 2023." April 2024. https://fdiinsider.com/news/significant-decline-in-foreign-direct-investment-in-asia-in-2023.

Ferguson, Niall. Empire: The Rise and Demise of the British World Order. Basic Books, 2003.

Ferreri, Joshua, Roger D. Peng, Michelle L. Bell, Ya Liu, Tiantian Li, and G. Brooke Anderson. "The January 2013 Beijing 'Airpocalypse' and Its Acute Effects on Emergency and Outpatient Visits at a Beijing Hospital." *Air Quality, Atmosphere & Health* 11, no. 3 (2017): 301–09. https://doi.org/10.1007/s11869-017-0538-0.

Financial Times. "EU Launches Two Probes into China Solar Manufacturers." April 3, 2024. https://www.ft.com/content/5e677032-82c6-4761-9053-a441ef1a71c4.

Flaaen, Aaron, Ali Hortaçsu, and Felix Tintelnot. "The Production Relocation and Price Effects of US Trade Policy: The Case of Washing Machines." *American Economic Review* 110, no. 7 (2020): 2103–127. https://www.aeaweb.org/articles?id=10.1257/aer.20190611.

"Free Trade," IGM Forum, University of Chicago Booth School of Business, March 13, 2012, http://www.igmchicago.org/surveys/free-trade.

Friedman, Milton, and Rose Friedman. *Free to Choose: A Personal Statement*. Harcourt Brace Jovanovich, 1980.

Fukuyama, Francis. *The Origins of Political Order*. Farrar, Straus and Giroux, 2011.

Gardner, Matthew. *Fortune 500 Companies Hold a Record $2.6 Trillion Offshore*. Institute on Taxation and Economic Policy, 2017. https://itep.org/wp-content/uploads/pre0327.pdf.

General Motors. *Annual Report 2010*. General Motors, 2010.

Germany Trade & Invest. "German Solar Market Doubled in 2010." *Solar Daily*. February 28, 2011.

Giles, John, Albert Park, and Juwei Zhang. "What Is China's True Unemployment Rate?" *China Economic Review* 16, no. 2 (2005): 149–70. https://doi.org/10.1016/j.chieco.2004.11.002.

Global Carbon Atlas. "CO2 Emissions by Country." 2023. https://globalcarbonatlas.org/emissions/carbon-emissions/.

Global Times. "U.S. Democracy in Crisis Makes Its Moral Teaching Hollow." Editorial. January 13, 2021.

Gordon, John Steele. "RE: A Significant Letter." *Commentary*. November 15, 2010. https://www.commentary.org/john-steele-gordon/re-a-significant-letter-2.

Greenstone, Michael, Guojun He, Tianyi Liu, and Nicholas Zhou. "Four Years After Declaring War on Pollution, China Is Winning." *Energy Policy Institute at the University of Chicago*. March 12, 2018. https://epic.uchicago.edu/research/four-years-after-declaring-war-on-pollution-china-is-winning/.

Haygood, Daniel M., and Glen W. Scott. "Henry Luce's American and Chinese Century: An Analysis of US News Magazines' Coverage of General Chiang Kai-shek from 1936 to 1949." *American Journalism* 38, no. 1 (2021).

Hicks, Michael, and Srikant Devaraj. *The Myth and the Reality of Manufacturing in America*. Ball State University, Center for Business and Economic Research, 2015. https://conexus.cberdata.org/files/MfgReality.pdf.

Hilton, Isabel. "How China Became the World's Leader on Renewable Energy." Yale School of the Environment. March 13, 2024. https://e360.yale.edu/features/china-renewable-energy.

Huang, Ray. 1587, A Year of No Significance: The Ming Dynasty in Decline. Yale University Press, 1981.

Hufbauer, Gary Clyde, and Euigin Jung. *Steel Profits Gain, but Steel Users Pay, Under Trump's Protectionism.* Peterson Institute for International Economics. December 2019.

Hufbauer, Gary Clyde, and Sean Lowry. *US Tire Tariffs: Saving Few Jobs at High Cost.* Peterson Institute for International Economics, 2012.

Huld, Arendse, and Qian Zhou. "China Manufacturing Industry Tracker." *China Briefing.* October 30, 2025. https://www.china-briefing.com/news/china-manufacturing-industry-tracker-2024-25/.

IndexMundi. "Japan - GDP per Capita." https://www.indexmundi.com/facts/japan/gdp-per-capita.

Institute of International Education. *Open Doors 2023 Report on International Educational Exchange,* 2023.

Institute of International Education. "United States Hosts Over 1 Million International Students, Fastest Enrollment Growth Rate in More Than 40 Years." Press release. November 13, 2023. https://www.iie.org/news/us-hosts-over-1-million-fastest-growth-for-40-years/.

International Energy Agency. *Energy Technology Perspectives 2023*, 2023. https://www.iea.org/reports/energy-technology-perspectives-2023.

International Energy Agency. *Global EV Outlook 2025: Electric Vehicle Batteries*, 2025. https://www.iea.org/reports/global-ev-outlook-2025/electric-vehicle-batteries.

International Energy Agency. *Renewables 2023: Executive Summary*, 2023. https://www.iea.org/reports/renewables-2023/executive-summary.

International Energy Agency. *Renewable Energy Medium-Term Market Report 2016: Market Analysis and Forecasts to 2021*. Paris: IEA, 2016.

International Renewable Energy Agency. *Renewable Power Generation Costs in 2020*, 2021. https://www.irena.org/publications/2021/Jun/Renewable-Power-Costs-in-2020.

International Trade Administration. "Jobs Supported by Exports 2022." US Department of Commerce. https://www.trade.gov/feature-article/otea-publications.

Irwin, Douglas A. *Free Trade Under Fire*. Princeton University Press, 2020.

Jing, Chai. *Under the Dome*. Documentary film. Released February 28, 2015.

Jinping, Xi. "Full Text: Speech by Xi Jinping at a Ceremony Marking the Centenary of the CPC." Speech transcript. *Global Times*, July 1, 2021. https://www.globaltimes.cn/page/202107/1227574.shtml.

Jinping, Xi. Report at 19th CPC National Congress. Xinhua, October 18, 2017. http://www.xinhuanet.com/english/download/Xi_Jinping's_report_at_19th_CPC_National_Congress.pdf.

Jinping, Xi. Speech at the Fifth Plenary Session of the 19th Central Committee. Xinhua, October 2020. https://www.xinhuanet.com/english/2020-10/29/c_139474610.htm.

Jisheng, Yang. *Tombstone: The Great Chinese Famine, 1958–1962*. Translated by Stacy Mosher and Guo Jian. Farrar, Straus and Giroux, 2012.

"Jobs Supported by Exports 2022." International Trade Administration. https://www.trade.gov/feature-article/otea-publications.

Johnson, Steve. "S&P 500 Trackers Hit a Record 27% of 2023 Equity ETF Flows." *Financial Times*. April 2, 2024. https://www.ft.com/content/4a9b70d7-f956-4ac7-b730-7ee3cafbd9e1.

Jones, Nicola. "China Tops CO_2 Emissions." *Nature*. June 20, 2007. https://www.nature.com/news/2007/070618/full/news070618-9.html.

Keller, Franklin Eric. "The United States and Industrial Policy: A Look Inside the CHIPS Program Office." Master's thesis, Harvard University Division of Continuing Education, 2025. https://dash.harvard.edu/server/api/core/bitstreams/5de6b5d8-e147-415b-ac15-6daef7e035f8/content.

Kerry, John. "Climate Diplomacy and the US-China Relationship." *Foreign Affairs*, September 2022.

Kissinger, Henry. *On China*. Penguin Press, 2011.

Kratz, Agatha, Camille Boullenois, and Jeremy Smith. "Why Isn't Europe Diversifying from China?" Rhodium Group. December 2, 2024. https://rhg.com/research/why-isnt-europe-diversifying-from-china.

Krugman, Paul. "How to Think About Trade Imbalance." Interview by Markus' Academy. January 30, 2025. https://economics.princeton.edu/wp-content/uploads/2025/01/2025.01.30-MA-Paul-Krugman.pdf.

Labor Force Characteristics by Race and Ethnicity, 2023. Report 1109. Bureau of Labor Statistics, 2024. https://www.bls.gov/opub/reports/race-and-ethnicity/2023/#:~:text=groups%20in%202023.-,Composition%20of%20the%20labor%20force,(See%20table%201.).

Lardy, Nicholas R. *The State Strikes Back: The End of Economic Reform in China?* Peterson Institute for International Economics, 2019.

Lelieveld, Jos, John S. Evans, Mihalis Fnais, Daniel Giannadaki, and Andrea Pozzer. "The Contribution of Outdoor Air Pollution Sources to Premature Mortality on a Global Scale." *Nature* 525 (2015): 367–71. https://doi.org/10.1038/nature15371.

Li, Alice. "China's Youth-Unemployment Pressure Eases as Index Falls for Third Straight Month." *South China Morning Post*. December 19, 2024. https://www.scmp.com/economy/economic-indicators/article/3291510/chinas-youth-unemployment-pressure-eases-index-falls-third-straight-month.

Li, Keqiang. "Remarks at the World Economic Forum Annual Meeting (Summer Davos)." Speech, Tianjin, June 26, 2015. *China Daily* and Ministry of Foreign Affairs of the PRC.

Lighthizer, Robert. "The Era of Offshoring U.S. Jobs Is Over." *The New York Times*, May 11, 2020. https://www.nytimes.com/2020/05/11/opinion/coronavirus-jobs-offshoring.html.

Lockheed Martin. "F-35 Lightning II: Global Partnership." Company factsheet. 2023. https://www.lockheedmartin.com/en-us/products/f-35/f-35-global-partnership.html.

Luce, Henry. "The American Century." *Life*, February 17, 1941.

Luce, Henry R. "The China Tragedy." *Life*, May 22, 1950.

Lutnick, Howard. Interview by Margaret Brennan. *Face the Nation with Margaret Brennan*, April 6, 2025. Transcript at https://www.cbsnews.com/news/transcript-commerce-secretary-howard-lutnick-on-face-the-nation-with-margaret-brennan-april-6-2025.

Lutz, Jessie, Gregory. *China and the Christian Colleges, 1850–1950.* Cornell University Press, 1971.

Macrotrends. "Japan GDP per Capita." https://www.macrotrends.net/global-metrics/countries/JPN/japan/gdp-per-capita.

Macrotrends. "South Korea GDP per Capita." https://www.macrotrends.net/global-metrics/countries/KOR/south-korea/gdp-per-capita.

McCarthy, Joseph R. Senate floor speech. March 30, 1950. Congressional Record, 81st Cong., 2nd sess., 96: 1461–464.

McDougall, Walter A. *Promised Land, Crusader State: The American Encounter with the World Since 1776.* Houghton Mifflin, 1997.

Melville, Herman. *Moby-Dick; or, The Whale.* 2nd ed. Edited by Harrison Hayford and Hershel Parker. W. W. Norton, 2002.

Mencius. *Mencius.* Translated by D. C. Lau. Penguin Classics, 1970.

Ministry of Environmental Protection of China. *2011 Report on the State of the Environment in China,* 2012. https://english.mee.gov.cn/News_service/news_release/201306/t20130607_253508.shtml.

Minton, Robbie, and Mariano Somale. "Detecting Tariff Effects on Consumer Prices in Real Time." Board of Governors of the Federal Reserve System, May 9, 2025. https://www.federalreserve.gov/econres/notes/feds-notes/detecting-tariff-effects-on-consumer-prices-in-real-time-20250509.html.

Morgan, Stephen, Shawn Arita, Jayson Beckman, Saquib Ahsan, Dylan Russell, Philip Jarrell, et al. "The Economic Impacts of Retaliatory Tariffs on US Agriculture." *US Department of Agriculture Economic Research Service.* November 1, 2022. https://ers.usda.gov/publications/pub-details/?pubid=102979.

Myers, Gustavus. *History of the Great American Fortunes.* Vol. 1. Charles H. Kerr & Company, 1910.

National Bureau of Statistics of China. "China's Foreign Exchange Reserves Reached USD 3.238 Trillion at the End of 2023." Press release. February 28, 2024. https://www.stats.gov.cn/english/PressRelease/202402/t20240228_1947918.html.

National Bureau of Statistics of China. "Industrial Production Operation in April 2025." May 26, 2025.

Navarro, Peter. *Death by China: Confronting the Dragon.* Prentice Hall, 2011.

Nordstrom, Anna. "The Important Role of the Foreign Investor in the U.S. Treasury Market." *Federal Reserve Bank of New York,* November

16, 2023. https://www.newyorkfed.org/newsevents/speeches/2023/nor231116.

Office of the United States Trade Representative. "2018 National Trade Estimate Report on Foreign Trade Barriers." March 30, 2018. https://ustr.gov/about-us/policy-offices/press-office/fact-sheets/2018/march/ustr-releases-2018-national-trade.

Oi, Jean C. Rural China Takes Off: Institutional Foundations of Economic Reform. University of California Press, 1999.

Organisation for Economic Co-operation and Development. *OECD Economic Outlook*, June 7, 2023. https://www.oecd.org/content/dam/oecd/en/publications/reports/2023/06/oecd-economic-outlook-volume-2023-issue-1_62ef0395/ce188438-en.pdf.

Organisation for Economic Co-operation and Development. *Industrial Subsidies and State Support in China*. Paris: OECD, 2019.

Pacheco, Marta. "China Dominating Soaring Global Clean-Tech Industry." *Euronews*. May 6, 2024. https://www.euronews.com/green/2024/05/06/china-dominating-soaring-global-clean-tech-industry.

Parrish, Meagan. "The Country with the Most FDA Warning Letters in 2019." Pharma Manufacturing. January 20, 2020. https://www.pharmamanufacturing.com/facilities/facility-design-management/article/11299227/the-country-with-the-most-fda-warning-letters-in-2019.

Payosova, Tetyana, Gary Clyde Hufbauer, and Jeffrey J. Schott. *The Dispute Settlement Crisis in the World Trade Organization: Causes and Cures*. Policy Brief 18-5. Peterson Institute for International Economics, 2018. https://www.piie.com/publications/policy-briefs/dispute-settlement-crisis-world-trade-organization-causes-and-cures.

Pei, Minxin. *China's Trapped Transition*. Harvard University Press, 2006.

Perkins, Tony. "Confronting Another Evil Empire: China." *Family Research Council.* December 7, 2021. https://www.frc.org/updatearticle/20211207/confronting-china.

Perry, Elizabeth J. *China's Governance in the "New Era" of Xi Jinping.* Cambridge University Press, 2021. https://elizabethperry.scholars.harvard.edu/sites/g/files/omnuum8556/files/chinas-governance-in-the-new-era-of-xi-jinping_1.pdf.

Perry, Elizabeth J. "China in Xi's 'New Era': The Return to Personalistic Rule." *Journal of Democracy* 30, no. 1 (2019): 22–36.

Pettis, Michael (@michaelxpettis). "Total debt as a share of GDP hit 295% in China last September, surpassing 257% in the US and an average of 258% in the eurozone." Twitter (now X). June 30, 2023. https://x.com/michaelxpettis/status/1668414476201373697.

Pettis, Michael. *Trade Wars Are Class Wars.* Yale University Press, 2020.

PharmaShots. "Top 20 R&D Spending Biopharma Companies of 2024." August 22, 2024, https://pharmashots.com/18880/top-20-r-d-spending-biopharma-companies-of-2024.

PhRMA. "Research and Development Expenditure of Total U.S. Pharmaceutical Industry from 1995 to 2023 (in Billion U.S. Dollars)." Chart. Statista, August 16, 2024. https://www.statista.com/statistics/265085/research-and-development-expenditure-us-pharmaceutical-industry/.

Pierson, Paul. "Increasing Returns, Path Dependence, and the Study of Politics." *American Political Science Review* 94, no. 2 (2000): 251–67.

Platt, Stephen R. Autumn in the Heavenly Kingdom: China, the West, and the Epic Story of the Taiping Civil War. Alfred A. Knopf, 2012.

Pliny the Elder. "Natural History." In *The History of Silk, Cotton, Linen, Wool, and Other Fibrous Substances.* Edited by Clinton G. Gilroy. Project Gutenberg, 2021.

Polo, Marco. *The Travels of Marco Polo*. Translated by Henry Yule. John Murray, 1875.

Preston, Andrew. Sword of the Spirit, Shield of Faith: Religion in American War and Diplomacy. Alfred A. Knopf, 2012.

Qichao, Liang. "Lun jiaohui zhi zhiye" [On the Activities of the Missionaries], *Shiwu bao* [*The Current Affairs Journal*], no. 22 (1896). Reprinted in *Liang Qichao quanji* [*The Collected Works of Liang Qichao*]. Vol. 2. Zhonghua Shuju, 1989.

Rajah, Roland, and Ahmed Albayrak. "China Versus America on Global Trade." *Lowy Institute*. January 2025. https://interactives.lowyinstitute.org/features/china-versus-america-on-global-trade/.

Rawski, Thomas G. "Chinese Dominance of Treaty Port Commerce and Its Implications, 1860–1875." *Explorations in Economic History* 7, no. 1–2 (1969): 451–73. https://sites.pitt.edu/~tgrawski/papers/1971%20Chinese%20Dominance%20ofTreaty%20Port%20Commerce.pdf.

Raymond, Nate. "BNP Paribas Sentenced in $8.9 Billion Accord over Sanctions Violations." *Reuters*. May 1, 2015. https://www.reuters.com/article/business/bnp-paribas-sentenced-in-89-billion-accord-over-sanctions-violations-idUSKBN0NM41J.

Reagan, Ronald. "Radio Address to the Nation on Free and Fair Trade." *Ronald Reagan Presidential Library & Museum*, September 13, 1986. https://www.reaganlibrary.gov/archives/speech/radio-address-nation-free-and-fair-trade-1.

Reid, Tim, and Gram Slattery. "Republican Presidential Hopeful Pence Says China Close to Becoming 'Evil Empire.'" *Reuters*. September 18, 2023. https://www.reuters.com/world/republican-presidential-hopeful-pence-says-china-close-becoming-evil-empire-2023-09-18.

Rubin, Robert. "China WTO Accession Will Require 'Real Market Opening.'" Press conference. US Department of State, Beijing.

September 26, 1999. https://usinfo.org/usia/usinfo.state.gov/regional/ea/uschina/rubin926.htm.

Rubio, Marco. "At Their Own Peril, Countries Embrace China." Press release. *US Senate Committee on Small Business & Entrepreneurship*, April 25, 2019. https://www.sbc.senate.gov/public/index.cfm/2019/4/marco-rubio-at-their-own-peril-countries-embrace-china.

Rubio, Marco. "Opening Remarks Before the Senate Foreign Relations Committee." Washington, DC. January 15, 2025. https://china.usembassy-china.org.cn/opening-remarks-by-secretary-of-state-designate-marco-rubio-before-the-senate-foreign-relations-committee.

Runde, Daniel F. "Enabling a Better Offer: How Does the West Counter Belt and Road?" Congressional testimony. *Center for Strategic and International Studies*, May 16, 2024. https://www.csis.org/analysis/enabling-better-offer-how-does-west-counter-belt-and-road.

"S&P 500 Q4 2018 Buybacks Set 4th Consecutive Quarterly Record at $223 Billion; 2018 Sets Record $806 Billion." *PR Newswire.* March 25, 2019. https://www.prnewswire.com/news-releases/sp-500-q4-2018-buybacks-set-4th-consecutive-quarterly-record-at-223-billion-2018-sets-record-806-billion-300817734.html.

Sanders, Bernie. Statement on trade policy. Congressional Record 161, no. 80 (May 22, 2015): S3321.

Sanger, David E., and Nicole Perlroth. "Chinese Army Unit Is Seen as Tied to Hacking Against U.S. Companies." *The New York Times*, February 18, 2013.

Sanket Koul. "IQVIA Institute: Indian Pharmaceutical Companies Supplied 47% of All Generic Prescriptions in US in 2022." *Business Standard.* May 17, 2024. https://www.business-standard.com/industry/news/indian-pharma-firms-supplied-47-of-all-generic-prescriptions-in-us-in-2022-124051701222_1.html.

Senate Democratic Leader Chuck Schumer. "Schumer: New Record Trade Deficit Indicates a Slow Bleeding at the Wrists for US Economy, Shows Increasing Dependence on Countries Like China, Japan." US Senate press release. July 25, 2006. https://www.schumer.senate.gov/newsroom/press-releases/schumer-new-record-trade-deficit-indicates-a-slow-bleeding-at-the-wrists-for-us-economy-shows-increasing-dependence-on-countries-like-china-japan.

Service v. Dulles, 354 US 363 (1957).

Service, John S. "Democratic Practices in Communist Areas." Report no. 20, enclosure no. 2. August 25, 1944. Records of the Department of State, National Archives, Washington, DC.

Service, John S. "First Informal Impressions of the North Shensi Communist Base." Foreign Relations of the United States: Diplomatic Papers, US Department of State, China, vol. VI, no. 1 (July 28, 1944): 517–20.

Service, John S. "Interview with Mao Tse-tung." Foreign Relations of the United States: Diplomatic Papers, US Department of State, Yenan, vol. VI, no. 15 (August 27, 1944).

Service, John S. "The Amerasia Papers: Some Problems in the History of US-China Relations." In *China Research Monographs*, no. 7. Center for Chinese Studies, University of California, 1971.

Service, John S. "The Communist Position." Report no. 5. August 3, 1944. Records of the Department of State, National Archives, Washington, DC.

Seward, William Henry. "Commerce in the Pacific Ocean." Speech before the US Senate. July 29, 1852. Quoted on plaque at Seward statue, Volunteer Park, Seattle.

Shultz, George P. "Remarks by Secretary of State George Shultz During Press Briefing on the President's Meeting with Soviet Foreign Minister

Shevardnadze." US Department of State. October 24, 1985. https://dp.la/item/057c68a28946331c8d29248a89ddc51a.

Silver, Laura, et al. "Unfavorable Views of China Reach Historic Highs in Many Countries." Pew Research Center. June 29, 2023.

Smith, Adam. In *An Inquiry into the Nature and Causes of the Wealth of Nations*. Edited by Edwin Cannan. Liberty Fund, 1981.

Solar PV Global Supply Chains. International Energy Agency, 2022. https://www.iea.org/reports/solar-pv-global-supply-chains.

Starbucks Corporation. "Starbucks Corporation, Starbucks Company Timeline: 2010–2017." https://about.starbucks.com/uploads/2023/02/AboutUs-Company-Timeline-2.6.23.pdf.

State Administration of Foreign Exchange. "Rules and Regulations." 2023. https://www.safe.gov.cn/en/RulesandRegulations/index.html.

State Council of the People's Republic of China. "China's Foreign Trade Surpasses 43 Trillion Yuan in 2022." *English.gov.cn*, February 7, 2025. https://english.www.gov.cn/archive/statistics/202502/07/content_WS67a5c74dc6d0868f4e8ef714.html.

State Council of the People's Republic of China. "China's High-Speed Rail Network Reaches 42,000 Kilometers." *English.gov.cn*, December 9, 2023. https://english.www.gov.cn/news/202312/09/content_WS6573b9bec6d0868f4e8e2045.html.

Stilwell, Joseph W. *The Stilwell Papers*. Edited by Theodore H. White. William Sloane Associates, 1948.

Subramanian, Vedant. "International Trade Tariffs Past and Present: A Review of Historical and 2025 US Tariff Impacts on Inflation, Consumption, Reshoring, and Substitution." *SSRN*, July 5, 2025. https://papers.ssrn.com/sol3/papers.cfm?abstract_id=5438034.

Sullivan, Jake. "Remarks at the Special Competitive Studies Project Global Emerging Technologies Summit." September 16, 2022. https://bidenwhitehouse.archives.gov/briefing-room/speeches-remarks/2022/09/16/remarks-by-national-security-advisor-jake-sullivan-at-the-special-competitive-studies-project-global-emerging-technologies-summit.

Tandon, Vaibhav. "Looking Back on the Smoot-Hawley Tariffs." *Northern Trust.* April 11, 2025. https://www.northerntrust.com/united-states/insights-research/2025/weekly-economic-commentary/looking-back-on-the-smoot-hawley-tariffs#:~:text=Upon%20ratification%20of%20the%20Smoot,over%20the%20same%20time%20period.

The Economist Intelligence Unit. "China's Demographic Outlook and Implications for 2035." January 30, 2024. https://www.eiu.com/n/chinas-demographic-outlook-and-implications-for-2035.

The White House. *National Security Strategy,* 2022. https://bidenwhitehouse.archives.gov/wp-content/uploads/2022/10/Biden-Harris-Administrations-National-Security-Strategy-10.2022.pdf.

"Trump Tweets: 'Trade Wars Are Good, and Easy to Win.'" *Reuters.* March 2, 2018. https://www.reuters.com/article/business/trump-tweets-trade-wars-are-good-and-easy-to-win-idUSKCN1GE1E9.

Tucker, Ruth A. From Jerusalem to Irian Jaya: A Biographical History of Christian Missions. 2nd ed. Zondervan, 2004.

United Nations Industrial Development Organization. *World Manufacturing Production: Annual Report 2022,* 2023. https://stat.unido.org/publications/world-manufacturing-production-report.

United Nations Statistics Division. "Trade of Goods, All Commodities: China Export Statistics, 2001–2021." *UN Comtrade Database.* https://data.un.org/Data.aspx?d=ComTrade&f=_l1Code%3A1%3BrtCode%3A156&q=China+datamart%5BComTrade%5D.

US Bureau of Economic Analysis and United States Census Bureau. "U.S. International Trade in Goods and Services: Annual Revision." News release, 2023. https://www.bea.gov/sites/default/files/2024-06/trad1324.pdf.

US Bureau of Economic Analysis. "U.S. International Trade in Goods and Services, December and Annual 2024." News release. Last modified February 5, 2025. https://www.bea.gov/news/2025/us-international-trade-goods-and-services-december-and-annual-2024.

US Bureau of Economic Analysis. "International Trade in Goods and Services." February 2024. https://www.bea.gov/data/intl-trade-investment/international-trade-goods-and-services.

US Department of Agriculture. "China Phase One Agreement." February 2020. https://www.fas.usda.gov/topics/china-phase-one-agreement.

US Department of Agriculture, Foreign Agricultural Service. "Global Agricultural Trade System." https://apps.fas.usda.gov/gats/.

US Department of Agriculture, Foreign Agricultural Service. "US Agricultural Exports Close 2024 on a Strong Note." February 26, 2025. https://www.fas.usda.gov/data/trade-spotlight-us-agricultural-exports-close-2024-on-strong-note.

US Department of Homeland Security Office of Homeland Security Statistics. "2020 Yearbook of Immigration Statistics." 2020. https://ohss.dhs.gov/topics/immigration/yearbook/2020.

US Department of Justice. "U.S. Charges Five Chinese Military Hackers for Cyber Espionage Against U.S. Corporations and a Labor Organization." News release. May 19, 2014.

US Department of State. *Foreign Relations of the United States: Diplomatic Papers, 1936, Volume IV: The Far East.* Washington, DC: Government Printing Office, 1954.

US Department of the Treasury. "US Foreign Aid to China, 1937–1945." Records of the Department of the Treasury, National Archives, Washington, DC.

US Government Accountability Office. "COVID-19: Opportunities to Improve Federal Response and Recovery Efforts." June 25, 2020. https://www.gao.gov/products/gao-20-625.

US International Trade Commission. "Cast Iron Pipe Fittings from China." Investigation Nos. 731-TA-278 and 731-TA-1064 (2003, with 2024 updates), https://www.usitc.gov/publications/701_731/pub5576.pdf.

"US Lawmakers Seek to Block Chinese Firms from Solar Manufacturing Subsidy." *Reuters*. July 31, 2024. https://www.reuters.com/business/energy/us-lawmakers-seek-block-chinese-firms-solar-manufacturing-subsidy-2024-07-31.

US Naval Institute. "Yankees in China Ports." *Proceedings*, October 1972, 836.

"US Tariffs: What's the Impact?" J.P. Morgan Global Research. October 30, 2025. https://www.jpmorgan.com/insights/global-research/current-events/us-tariffs.

US Trade Representative. *2020 Report to Congress on China's WTO Compliance*. Washington, DC: Office of the US Trade Representative, 2021.

Vine, David. Base Nation: How US Military Bases Abroad Harm America and the World. Metropolitan Books, Henry Holt and Company, 2015.

Vogel, Ezra F. *Deng Xiaoping and the Transformation of China*. Harvard University Press, 2011.

Walsh, Matt. "This Might Be the Most Orwellian Law I've Ever Heard Of." *Daily Wire*. April 10, 2025. https://www.dailywire.com/news/this-might-be-the-most-orwellian-law-ive-ever-heard-of.

Wang, Hui. "The Politics of Imagining Asia." *Inter-Asia Cultural Studies* 8, no. 1 (2007): 1–33.

Wang, Zheng. Never Forget National Humiliation: Historical Memory in Chinese Politics and Foreign Relations. Columbia University Press, 2012.

Warren, Elizabeth. "In Bipartisan Letter, Warren, Cotton, Kaine, & Romney Warn of National Security and Public Health Risks Posed by China's Influence over Drug Supply." Letter posted on office website. December 9, 2019. https://www.warren.senate.gov/oversight/letters/in-bipartisan-letter-warren-cotton-kaine-and-romney-warn-of-national-security-and-public-health-risks-posed-by-chinas-influence-over-drug-supply-chain.

"Where We Stand: The Fiscal, Economic, and Distributional Effects of All US Tariffs." The Budget Lab at Yale. April 2, 2025. https://budgetlab.yale.edu/research/where-we-stand-fiscal-economic-and-distributional-effects-all-us-tariffs-enacted-2025-through-april.

World Bank Group. "GDP (Current US$)—China." https://data.worldbank.org/indicator/NY.GDP.MKTP.CD?locations=CN.

World Bank Group. "Life Expectancy at Birth, Total (Years)—China." https://data.worldbank.org/indicator/SP.DYN.LE00.IN?locations=CN.

World Bank Group. "The World Bank in China: Overview." Last updated October 23, 2024. https://www.worldbank.org/en/country/china/overview.

World Bank Group. "The World Bank in Viet Nam: Overview." Last updated May 9, 2025. https://www.worldbank.org/en/country/vietnam/overview.

World Bank Group. Four Decades of Poverty Reduction in China: Drivers, Insights for the World, and the Way Ahead, 2022.

World Bank Group. *Poverty and Shared Prosperity 2020: Reversals of Fortune*, 2020. https://www.worldbank.org/en/publication/poverty-and-shared-prosperity.

World Bank Group. *Poverty and Shared Prosperity 2022: Correcting Course*, 2022. https://www.worldbank.org.

World Bank Group. *Russia Economic Report No. 33*. World Bank, 2015. https://www.worldbank.org/content/dam/Worldbank/document/eca/russia/rer33-eng.pdf.

World Bank Group. *World Development Report 2020: Trading for Development in the Age of Global Value Chains.* World Bank, 2019. https://www.worldbank.org/en/publication/wdr2020.

World Intellectual Property Organization. *WIPO IP Facts and Figures: China 2020.* Geneva: WIPO, 2020.

World Trade Organization. *Subsidies and Countervailing Measures Agreement and China Notifications.* Geneva: WTO, 2020.

World Wind Energy Association. *WWEA Annual Report 2023: Record Year for Windpower*, 2024. https://www.wwindea.org/AnnualReport2023.

Wynne-Jones, Steve. "China Set to Record $2.2T in E-Commerce Sales in 2023: Report." *ESM Magazine*. September 1, 2023. https://www.esm-magazine.com/technology/china-set-to-record-2-2tn-in-e-commerce-sales-in-2023-report-248670.

Xiaohuan, Lan. How China Works: An Introduction to China's State-led Economic Development. Palgrave Macmillan, 2024.

Yao, Kevin, and Ellen Zhang. "China Revises Up 2023 GDP, Sees Little Impact on 2024 Growth." *Reuters*. December 26, 2024. https://www.reuters.com/world/china/china-revises-up-2023-gdp-1773-trillion-2024-12-26.

York, Erica, and Alex Durante. "Trump Tariffs: The Economic Impact of the Trump Trade War." *Tax Foundation*. Last updated November 17, 2025. https://taxfoundation.org/research/all/federal/trump-tariffs-trade-war.

Yousef, Abraham. "The Latest Trends on Social Media Apps - Q1 2023." *Sensor Tower* (blog). April 2023. https://sensortower.com/blog/the-latest-trends-on-social-media-apps-q1-2023.

Zeihan, Peter. "Don't Be Surprised by China's Collapse." *Zeihan on Geopolitics*. September 19, 2023. https://zeihan.com/dont-be-surprised-by-chinas-collapse.

Zuo, Mandy. "China's Middle-Income Population Passes 500 Million Mark, State-Owned Newspaper Says." *South China Morning Post*. March 3, 2024. https://www.scmp.com/economy/china-economy/article/3253995/chinas-middle-income-population-passes-500-million-mark-says-state-owned-newspaper.

GLOBALIST
BRING JOBS HOME
NO MORE CHINA TRADE

ENDNOTES

1 "What Happened When China Joined the WTO?," Council on Foreign Relations, last updated February 6, 2025, https://education.cfr.org/learn/reading/what-happened-when-china-joined-wto.

2 "US–China Trade Stayed Robust in 2022. Will That Last?," *ChinaFile*, March 13, 2023, https://www.chinafile.com/conversation/us-china-trade-stayed-robust-2022-will-last.

3 Tim Reid and Gram Slattery, "Republican Presidential Hopeful Pence Says China Close to Becoming 'Evil Empire,'" *Reuters*, September 18, 2023, https://www.reuters.com/world/republican-presidential-hopeful-pence-says-china-close-becoming-evil-empire-2023-09-18.

4 Tom Cotton, "Seven Things You Can't Say About China," lecture presented at the Hudson Institute, Washington, DC, February 16, 2025, https://www.hudson.org/events/seven-things-you-cant-say-about-china-senator-tom-cotton-john-walters.

5 Tony Perkins, "Confronting Another Evil Empire: China," *Family Research Council*, December 7, 2021, https://www.frc.org/updatearticle/20211207/confronting-china.

6 "US Lawmakers Seek to Block Chinese Firms from Solar Manufacturing Subsidy," *Reuters*, July 31, 2024, https://www.reuters.com/business/

energy/us-lawmakers-seek-block-chinese-firms-solar-manufacturing-subsidy-2024-07-31.

7 Germany Trade & Invest, "German Solar Market Doubled in 2010," *Solar Daily*, February 28, 2011.

8 Ulrich Fahl, "German Energy Transition (Energiewende) and What Politicians Can Learn for Environmental and Climate Policy," *Clean Technologies and Environmental Policy* 22 (2020): 1834, https://link.springer.com/article/10.1007/s10098-020-01939-3.

9 International Energy Agency, *Renewable Energy Medium-Term Market Report 2016: Market Analysis and Forecasts to 2021* (Paris: IEA, 2016).

10 Emily Benson and Claire Y. Li, "China's New Economic Statecraft: Industrial Subsidies and Strategic Industries" (Center for Strategic and International Studies, 2023).

11 Savannah Bertrand, "Fact Sheet | Proposals to Reduce Fossil Fuel Subsidies (2021)," *Environmental and Energy Study Institute*, July 23, 2021, https://www.eesi.org/papers/view/fact-sheet-proposals-to-reduce-fossil-fuel-subsidies-2021.

12 Elizabeth Warren, "In Bipartisan Letter, Warren, Cotton, Kaine, & Romney Warn of National Security and Public Health Risks Posed by China's Influence over Drug Supply," letter posted on office website, December 9, 2019, https://www.warren.senate.gov/oversight/letters/in-bipartisan-letter-warren-cotton-kaine-and-romney-warn-of-national-security-and-public-health-risks-posed-by-chinas-influence-over-drug-supply-chain.

13 *Annual Report and Accounts 2022–23* (British Council, 2023), https://www.britishcouncil.org/sites/default/files/britishcouncil_annualreport_2022-23.pdf.

14 Kevin Yao and Ellen Zhang, "China Revises Up 2023 GDP, Sees Little Impact on 2024 Growth," *Reuters*,

December 26, 2024, https://www.reuters.com/world/china/china-revises-up-2023-gdp-1773-trillion-2024-12-26.

15 Pliny the Elder, "Natural History (11.78)," in *The History of Silk, Cotton, Linen, Wool, and Other Fibrous Substances*, ed. Clinton G. Gilroy (Project Gutenberg, 2021).

16 Marco Polo, *The Travels of Marco Polo*, Book 2, Part 1, trans. Henry Yule (John Murray, 1875).

17 US Naval Institute, "Yankees in China Ports," *Proceedings*, October 1972, 836.

18 William Henry Seward, "Commerce in the Pacific Ocean" (speech, US Senate, July 29, 1852), quoted on plaque at Seward statue, Volunteer Park, Seattle.

19 *Annual Report of the American Board of Commissioners for Foreign Missions*, vol. 51 (American Board of Commissioners for Foreign Missions, 1860), Yale Divinity Library digital collection, 49–51.

20 Gustavus Myers, *History of the Great American Fortunes*, vol. 1 (Charles H. Kerr & Company, 1910).

21 Walter A. McDougall, *Promised Land, Crusader State: The American Encounter with the World Since 1776* (Houghton Mifflin, 1997), 52–54.

22 Herman Melville, *Moby-Dick; or, The Whale*, eds. Harrison Hayford and Hershel Parker, 2nd ed. (W. W. Norton, 2002), 107.

23 Thomas G. Rawski, "Chinese Dominance of Treaty Port Commerce and Its Implications, 1860–1875," *Explorations in Economic History* 7, no. 1–2 (1969): 451–73, https://sites.pitt.edu/~tgrawski/papers/1971%20Chinese%20Dominance%20ofTreaty%20Port%20Commerce.pdf.

24 *Annual Report 2010* (General Motors, 2010), 36–37.

25 Starbucks Corporation, "*Starbucks Opens State-of-the-Art Premium Reserve Roastery Experience in Shanghai,*" press release, December 5, 2017

26 Apple Inc., *Form 10-K for the fiscal year ended September 25, 2021*, note "Segment Information and Geographic Data," net sales for "Greater China" US $68,366 million.

27 Mandy Zuo, "China's Middle-Income Population Passes 500 Million Mark, State-Owned Newspaper Says," *South China Morning Post*, March 3, 2024, https://www.scmp.com/economy/china-economy/article/3253995/chinas-middle-income-population-passes-500-million-mark-says-state-owned-newspaper.

28 Steve Wynne-Jones, "China Set to Record $2.2T in E-Commerce Sales in 2023: Report," *ESM Magazine*, September 1, 2023, https://www.esmmagazine.com/technology/china-set-to-record-2-2tn-in-e-commerce-sales-in-2023-report-248670.

29 State Council of the People's Republic of China, "China's High-Speed Rail Network Reaches 42,000 Kilometers," *English.gov.cn*, December 9, 2023, https://english.www.gov.cn/news/202312/09/content_WS6573b9bec6d0868f4e8e2045.html.

30 Stephen R. Platt, Autumn in the Heavenly Kingdom: China, the West, and the Epic Story of the Taiping Civil War (Alfred A. Knopf, 2012).

31 Andrew Preston, Sword of the Spirit, Shield of Faith: Religion in American War and Diplomacy (Alfred A. Knopf, 2012).

32 *Annual Report of the American Board of Commissioners for Foreign Missions, 1850* (American Board of Commissioners for Foreign Missions, 1850), Yale Divinity Library digital collection, 19.

33 John King Fairbank, *The Missionary Enterprise in China and America* (Harvard University Press, 1974).

34 Daniel M. Haygood and Glen W. Scott, "Henry Luce's American and Chinese Century: An Analysis of US News Magazines' Coverage of General Chiang Kai-shek from 1936 to 1949," *American Journalism* 38, no. 1 (2021).

35 Jessie Gregory Lutz, *China and the Christian Colleges, 1850–1950* (Cornell University Press, 1971).

36 Liang Qichao, "Lun jiaohui zhi zhiye" [On the Activities of the Missionaries], *Shiwu bao* [*The Current Affairs Journal]*, no. 22 (1896). Reprinted in *Liang Qichao quanji* [*The Collected Works of Liang Qichao*], vol. 2 (Zhonghua Shuju, 1989), 45–47.

37 Ruth A. Tucker, From Jerusalem to Irian Jaya: A Biographical History of Christian Missions, 2nd ed. (Zondervan, 2004).

38 *Annual Report: Religious Persecution Statistics, 2023* (ChinaAid, 2023), https://www.chinaaid.org/reports.

39 George P. Shultz, "Remarks by Secretary of State George Shultz During Press Briefing on the President's Meeting with Soviet Foreign Minister Shevardnadze" (US Department of State, October 24, 1985), https://dp.la/item/057c68a28946331c8d29248a89ddc51a.

40 Henry Luce, "The American Century," *Life*, February 17, 1941.

41 William J. Clinton, "Full Text of Clinton's Speech on China Trade Bill" (speech, Paul H. Nitze School of Advanced International Studies, Johns Hopkins University, March 8, 2000), https://www.iatp.org/sites/default/files/Full_Text_of_Clintons_Speech_on_China_Trade_Bi.htm.

42 Marco Rubio, "At Their Own Peril, Countries Embrace China," press release, *US Senate Committee on Small Business & Entrepreneurship*, April 25, 2019, https://www.sbc.senate.gov/public/index.cfm/2019/4/marco-rubio-at-their-own-peril-countries-embrace-china.

43 "Japan GDP per Capita," Macrotrends, https://www.macrotrends.net/global-metrics/countries/JPN/japan/gdp-per-capita.

44 "South Korea GDP per Capita," Macrotrends, https://www.macrotrends.net/global-metrics/countries/KOR/south-korea/gdp-per-capita.

45 Hui Wang, "The Politics of Imagining Asia," *Inter-Asia Cultural Studies* 8, no. 1 (2007): 1–33.

46 Dean Acheson, United States Relations with China: With Special Reference to the Period 1944–1949 (US Government Printing Office, 1949).

47 George W. Bush, "Transcript: Bush Describes U.S. Values to Chinese Students," transcript of remarks at Tsinghua University, February 22, 2002, https://usinfo.org/wf-archive/2002/020222/epf502.htm.

48 Elizabeth J. Perry, *China's Governance in the "New Era" of Xi Jinping* (Cambridge University Press, 2021), https://elizabethperry.scholars.harvard.edu/sites/g/files/omnuum8556/files/chinas-governance-in-the-new-era-of-xi-jinping_1.pdf; Elizabeth J. Perry, "China in Xi's 'New Era': The Return to Personalistic Rule," *Journal of Democracy* 30, no. 1 (2019): 22–36.

49 Minxin Pei, *China's Trapped Transition* (Harvard University Press, 2006).

50 Gordon Chang, *The Coming Collapse of China* (Random House, 2001).

51 Peter Zeihan, interview on *The Jay Martin Show*, YouTube video, 13:12 mark, published January 25, 2023, https://www.youtube.com/watch?v=fjFQQ5Q_U-A.

52 Xi Jinping, *"Xi Says Chinese People Will Never Allow Foreign Bullying, Oppressing, or Subjugating,"* Xinhua / Government of China, July 1, 2021, https://english.www.gov.cn/news/topnews/202107/01/content_WS60dd2ee2c6d0df57f98dc3ab.html

53 I-Chuan Wu-Beyens, "The Years of Reform in China: Economic Growth Versus Modernization," *Civilisations* 40, no. 1 (1992): 101-32, https://journals.openedition.org/civilisations/1680.

54 Yang Jisheng, *Tombstone: The Great Chinese Famine, 1958–1962*, trans. Stacy Mosher and Guo Jian (Farrar, Straus and Giroux, 2012).

55 "China Currently Dominates Global Solar PV Supply Chains," executive summary, International Energy Association, https://www.iea.org/reports/solar-pv-global-supply-chains/executive-summary.

56 World Bank, *Poverty and Shared Prosperity 2022: Correcting Course* (Washington, DC: World Bank, 2022), https://www.worldbank.org.

57 World Bank, "GDP per Capita (Current US$)–China," World Development Indicators, 2024, https://data.worldbank.org.

58 "Life Expectancy at Birth, Total (Years) - China, 2022," World Bank Group, https://data.worldbank.org/indicator/SP.DYN.LE00.IN?locations=CN.

59 "Correctly Viewing the Two Historical Periods Before and After Reform and Opening Up—Studying General Secretary Xi Jinping's Important Discussion on 'Two Things That Cannot Be Negated,'" *People's Daily*, November 8, 2013.

60 *Russia Economic Report No. 33* (World Bank Group, 2015), https://www.worldbank.org/content/dam/Worldbank/document/eca/russia/rer33-eng.pdf.

61 Jake Sullivan, "Remarks at the Special Competitive Studies Project Global Emerging Technologies Summit," September 16, 2022, https://bidenwhitehouse.archives.gov/briefing-room/speeches-remarks/2022/09/16/remarks-by-national-security-advisor-jake-sullivan-at-the-special-competitive-studies-project-global-emerging-technologies-summit.

62 Robert Rubin, "China WTO Accession Will Require 'Real Market Opening,'" press conference, US Department of State, Beijing, September 26, 1999, https://usinfo.org/usia/usinfo.state.gov/regional/ea/uschina/rubin926.htm.

63 Office of the United States Trade Representative, "2018 National Trade Estimate Report on Foreign Trade Barriers," March 30, 2018, https://ustr.gov/about-us/policy-offices/press-office/fact-sheets/2018/march/ustr-releases-2018-national-trade.

64 Chad P. Bown, "US-China Trade War Tariffs: An Up-to-Date Chart," *Peterson Institute for International Economics*, August 27, 2025, https://www.piie.com/research/piie-charts/2019/us-china-trade-war-tariffs-date-chart.

65 "Trump Tweets: 'Trade Wars Are Good, and Easy to Win,'" *Reuters*, March 2, 2018, https://www.reuters.com/article/business/trump-tweets-trade-wars-are-good-and-easy-to-win-idUSKCN1GE1E9.

66 Abraham Yousef, "The Latest Trends on Social Media Apps - Q1 2023," *Sensor Tower* (blog), April 2023, https://sensortower.com/blog/the-latest-trends-on-social-media-apps-q1-2023.

67 David Vine, *Base Nation: How US Military Bases Abroad Harm America and the World* (Metropolitan Books, Henry Holt and Company, 2015).

68 Tetyana Payosova et al., *The Dispute Settlement Crisis in the World Trade Organization: Causes and Cures*, Policy Brief 18-5 (Peterson Institute for International Economics, 2018), https://www.piie.com/publications/policy-briefs/dispute-settlement-crisis-world-trade-organization-causes-and-cures.

69 Nate Raymond, "BNP Paribas Sentenced in $8.9 Billion Accord over Sanctions Violations," *Reuters*, May 1, 2015, https://www.reuters.com/article/business/bnp-paribas-sentenced-in-89-billion-accord-over-sanctions-violations-idUSKBN0NM41J.

70 Daniel F. Runde, "Enabling a Better Offer: How Does the West Counter Belt and Road?," Congressional testimony, *Center for Strategic and International Studies*, May 16, 2024, https://www.csis.org/analysis/enabling-better-offer-how-does-west-counter-belt-and-road.

71 Xi Jinping, report at 19th CPC National Congress, Xinhua, October 18, 2017, http://www.xinhuanet.com/english/2017-10/18/c_136703314.htm.

72 Xi Jinping, *"Understanding the New Development Stage, Applying a New Development Philosophy,"* Qiushi, July 8, 2021, http://en.qstheory.cn/2021-07/08/c_641137.htm; Xi Jinping, addressing the fifth plenary session of the 19th CCP Central Committee, January 2021 (author's translation of his statement "East is rising, West is declining").

73 "GDP (current US$) - China," World Bank Group, https://data.worldbank.org/indicator/NY.GDP.MKTP.CD?locations=CN.

74 State Council of the People's Republic of China, "China's Foreign Trade Surpasses 43 Trillion Yuan in 2022," *English.gov.*cn, February 7, 2025, https://english.www.gov.cn/archive/statistics/202502/07/content_WS67a5c74dc6d0868f4e8ef714.html.

75 *World Manufacturing Production: Annual Report 2022* (United Nations Industrial Development Organization, 2023), https://stat.unido.org/publications/world-manufacturing-production-report.

76 National Bureau of Statistics of China, "China's Foreign Exchange Reserves Reached USD 3.238 Trillion at the End of 2023," press release, February 28, 2024, https://www.stats.gov.cn/english/PressRelease/202402/t20240228_1947918.html.

77 Jason W. Davidson, "The Costs of War to United States Allies Since 9/11," *Brown University*, May 12, 2021, https://costsofwar.watson.brown.edu/paper/costs-war-united-states-allies-911.

78 China Association of Automobile Manufacturers, "2024 Vehicle Sales of China," *Asian Automotive Analysis*, April 7, 2025, https://aaa.fourin.com/reports/0216b120-137a-11f0-a1e1-630064034eb7/2024-vehicle-sales-of-china.

79 *Renewables 2023: Executive Summary* (International Energy Agency, 2023), https://www.iea.org/reports/renewables-2023/executive-summary.

80 "COVID-19 Mortality," Centers for Disease Control and Prevention, National Center for Health Statistics, August 20, 2025, https://www.cdc.gov/nchs/state-stats/deaths/covid19.html.

81 "U.S. Democracy in Crisis Makes Its Moral Teaching Hollow," editorial, *Global Times*, January 13, 2021.

82 Li Keqiang, "Remarks at the World Economic Forum Annual Meeting (Summer Davos)" (speech, Tianjin, June 26, 2015), *China Daily* and Ministry of Foreign Affairs of the PRC.

83 Bloomberg, "China's Population Shrinks for First Time in Six Decades," *TIME*, January 17, 2023, https://time.com/6247641/china-population-decline-six-decades.

84 "China's Demographic Outlook and Implications for 2035," The Economist Intelligence Unit, January 30, 2024, https://www.eiu.com/n/chinas-demographic-outlook-and-implications-for-2035.

85 Michael Pettis (@michaelxpettis), "Total debt as a share of GDP hit 295% in China last September, surpassing 257% in the US and an average of 258% in the eurozone," Twitter (now X), June 30, 2023, https://x.com/michaelxpettis/status/1668414476201373697.

86 Alice Li, "China's Youth-Unemployment Pressure Eases as Index Falls for Third Straight Month," *South China Morning Post*, December 19, 2024, https://www.scmp.com/economy/economic-indicators/

article/3291510/chinas-youth-unemployment-pressure-eases-index-falls-third-straight-month.

87 "Significant Decline in Foreign Direct Investment in Asia in 2023," *FDI Insider*, April 2024, https://fdiinsider.com/news/significant-decline-in-foreign-direct-investment-in-asia-in-2023.

88 Matt Walsh, "This Might Be the Most Orwellian Law I've Ever Heard Of," *Daily Wire*, April 10, 2025, https://www.dailywire.com/news/this-might-be-the-most-orwellian-law-ive-ever-heard-of.

89 Walsh, "This Might Be the Most Orwellian Law."

90 John S. Service, "The Amerasia Papers: Some Problems in the History of US-China Relations," in *China Research Monographs*, no. 7 (Center for Chinese Studies, University of California, 1971), 220.

91 "Political Conditions in North China," Foreign Relations of the United States: Diplomatic Papers, US Department of State, The Far East, vol. IV, no. 552, Peiping (July 3, 1936): 231–40.

92 US Department of the Treasury, "US Foreign Aid to China, 1937–1945," Records of the Department of the Treasury, National Archives, Washington, DC.

93 Joseph W. Stilwell, *The Stilwell Papers*, ed. Theodore H. White (William Sloane Associates, 1948).

94 John S. Service, "First Informal Impressions of the North Shensi Communist Base," Foreign Relations of the United States: Diplomatic Papers, US Department of State, China, vol. VI, no. 1 (July 28, 1944): 517–20.

95 John S. Service, "Interview with Mao Tse-tung," Foreign Relations of the United States: Diplomatic Papers, US Department of State, Yenan, vol. VI, no. 15 (August 27, 1944).

96 John S. Service, "Democratic Practices in Communist Areas," report no. 20, enclosure no. 2, August 25, 1944, Records of the Department of State, National Archives, Washington, DC.

97 John S. Service, "The Communist Position," report no. 5, August 3, 1944, Records of the Department of State, National Archives, Washington, DC.

98 "Amerasia Case Summary," File 65-56402, 1945, Federal Bureau of Investigation Records, National Archives and Records Administration, Washington, DC.

99 Congressional Record, 81st Cong., 2nd sess., February 20, 1950, 96: 3452–56.

100 Joseph R. McCarthy, Senate floor speech, March 30, 1950, Congressional Record, 81st Cong., 2nd sess., 96: 1461–64.

101 Henry R. Luce, "The China Tragedy," *Life*, May 22, 1950.

102 Service v. Dulles, 354 US 363 (1957).

103 John King Fairbank, *The United States and China* (Harvard University Press, 1979).

104 Henry Kissinger, *On China* (Penguin Press, 2011).

105 Senator Marsha Blackburn (@MarshaBlackburn), "China has a 5,000 year history of cheating and stealing. Some things will never change ...," Twitter (now X), December 3, 2020, https://x.com/MarshaBlackburn/status/1334510812552163328.

106 Senator Marco Rubio, "Opening Remarks Before the Senate Foreign Relations Committee," Washington, DC, January 15, 2025, https://china.usembassy-china.org.cn/opening-remarks-by-secretary-of-state-designate-marco-rubio-before-the-senate-foreign-relations-committee.

107 "Taiwan GDP - Gross Domestic Product," countryeconomy.com, https://countryeconomy.com/gdp/taiwan. n.d.

108 "Japan - GDP per Capita," IndexMundi, https://www.indexmundi.com/facts/japan/gdp-per-capita.

109 countryeconomy.com, "Taiwan GDP."

110 countryeconomy.com, "Taiwan GDP."

111 Adam Smith, chap. II, book IV, in *An Inquiry into the Nature and Causes of the Wealth of Nations*, ed. Edwin Cannan (Liberty Fund, 1981), 456–57.

112 "Top 20 R&D Spending Biopharma Companies of 2024," PharmaShots, August 22, 2024. https://pharmashots.com/15371/top-20-rd-spending-biopharma-companies-of-2024

113 Statista, "U.S. pharmaceutical industry – R&D expenditure of total U.S. pharmaceutical industry from 1995 to 2023," *Statista*, August 2024, https://www.statista.com/statistics/265085/research-and-development-expenditure-us-pharmaceutical-industry/.

114 Sanket Koul, "Indian Pharma Firms Supplied 47% of All Generic Prescriptions in US in 2022," *Business Standard*, May 17, 2024, https://www.business-standard.com/industry/news/indian-pharma-firms-supplied-47-of-all-generic-prescriptions-in-us-in-2022-124051701222_1.html.

115 Meagan Parrish, "The Country with the Most FDA Warning Letters in 2019," Pharma Manufacturing, January 20, 2020, https://www.pharmamanufacturing.com/facilities/facility-design-management/article/11299227/the-country-with-the-most-fda-warning-letters-in-2019.

116 Toni Clarke, "India's Ranbaxy Hit by FDA Product Ban at Fourth Indian Plant," *Reuters*, January 24, 2014, https://www.reuters.com/

article/business/indias-ranbaxy-hit-by-fda-product-ban-at-4th-indian-plant-idUSBREA0N070/.

117 Milton Friedman and Rose Friedman, *Free to Choose: A Personal Statement* (Harcourt Brace Jovanovich, 1980), 22.

118 Howard Lutnick, interview by Margaret Brennan, *Face the Nation with Margaret Brennan*, April 6, 2025, transcript at https://www.cbsnews.com/news/transcript-commerce-secretary-howard-lutnick-on-face-the-nation-with-margaret-brennan-april-6-2025.

119 "U.S. Agricultural Exports Close 2024 on a Strong Note," Foreign Agricultural Service, US Department of Agriculture, February 26, 2025, https://www.fas.usda.gov/data/trade-spotlight-us-agricultural-exports-close-2024-on-strong-note.

120 Institute of International Education (IIE). *Open Doors 2023 Report on International Educational Exchange: United States Hosts Over 1 Million International Students, Fastest Enrollment Growth Rate in More Than 40 Years.* Press release, November 13, 2023. https://opendoorsdata.org/wp-content/uploads/2023/11/IIE_-Open-Doors-Press-Release-2023-2.pdf.

121 National Bureau of Statistics of China, National Economic Performance of Industrial Enterprises Above Designated Size, various years; World Bank, Global Value Chain Development Report (2017); OECD, Global Value Chains and Trade in Value Added (2013); and Kenneth L. Kraemer, Greg Linden, and Jason Dedrick, "Capturing Value in Global Value Chains: The Case of the iPhone," Communications of the ACM 54, no. 4 (2011): 36–44.

122 "U.S. International Trade in Goods and Services, December and Annual 2024," news release, US Bureau of Economic Analysis, last updated February 5, 2025, https://www.bea.gov/news/2025/us-international-trade-goods-and-services-december-and-annual-2024.

123 "Trade and American Jobs: The Impact of Trade on U.S. and State-Level Employment: 2022 Update," *Business Roundtable*, February 28, 2022, https://www.businessroundtable.org/trade-and-american-jobs-the-impact-of-trade-on-us-and-state-level-employment-2022-update.

124 "Jobs Supported by Exports 2022," OTEA Publications, International Trade Administration, https://www.trade.gov/feature-article/otea-publications.

125 Vaibhav Tandon, "Looking Back on the Smoot-Hawley Tariffs," *Northern Trust*, April 11, 2025, https://www.northerntrust.com/united-states/insights-research/2025/weekly-economic-commentary/looking-back-on-the-smoot-hawley-tariffs#:~:text=Upon%20ratification%20of%20the%20Smoot,over%20the%20same%20time%20period.

126 John Steele Gordon, "RE: A Significant Letter," *Commentary*, November 15, 2010, https://www.commentary.org/john-steele-gordon/re-a-significant-letter-2/.

127 Tandon, "Looking Back on the Smoot-Hawley Tariffs."

128 Tandon, "Looking Back on the Smoot-Hawley Tariffs."

129 Ronald Reagan, "Radio Address to the Nation on Free and Fair Trade," *Ronald Reagan Presidential Library & Museum*, September 13, 1986, https://www.reaganlibrary.gov/archives/speech/radio-address-nation-free-and-fair-trade-1.

130 Douglas A. Irwin, *Free Trade Under Fire* (Princeton University Press, 2020), 3.

131 "Free Trade," IGM Forum, University of Chicago Booth School of Business, March 13, 2012. https://www.igmchicago.org/surveys/free-trade/.

132 "Schumer: New Record Trade Deficit Indicates a Slow Bleeding at the Wrists for U.S. Economy, Shows Increasing Dependence on Countries Like China, Japan," Senate Democratic Leader Chuck Schumer, US Senate press release, July 25, 2006, https://www.schumer.senate.gov/newsroom/press-releases/schumer-new-record-trade-deficit-indicates-a-slow-bleeding-at-the-wrists-for-us-economy-shows-increasing-dependence-on-countries-like-china-japan.

133 "U.S. International Trade in Goods and Services," US Bureau of Economic Analysis, February 2024, https://www.bea.gov/data/intl-trade-investment/international-trade-goods-and-services.

134 Anna Nordstrom, "The Important Role of the Foreign Investor in the U.S. Treasury Market," Federal Reserve Bank of New York, November 16, 2023, https://www.newyorkfed.org/newsevents/speeches/2023/nor231116.

135 Paul Krugman, "How to Think About Trade Imbalances," interview by Markus' Academy, January 30, 2025, https://economics.princeton.edu/wp-content/uploads/2025/01/2025.01.30-MA-Paul-Krugman.pdf.

136 Michael Pettis, *Trade Wars Are Class Wars* (Yale University Press, 2020), 127.

137 *OECD Economic Outlook* (Organisation for Economic Co-operation and Development, 2023), https://www.oecd.org/content/dam/oecd/en/publications/reports/2023/06/oecd-economic-outlook-volume-2023-issue-1_62ef0395/ce188438-en.pdf.

138 Michael Pettis, *The Great Rebalancing: Trade, Conflict, and the Perilous Road Ahead for the World Economy* (Princeton University Press, 2013). See Chapter 3, esp. pp. 56–63.

139 State Administration of Foreign Exchange (SAFE). "Rules and Regulations: Annual Individual Quota for Foreign Exchange Purchase." SAFE.gov.cn, 2023. https://www.safe.gov.cn.

140 US Department of Justice, "U.S. Charges Five Chinese Military Hackers for Cyber Espionage Against U.S. Corporations and a Labor Organization," news release, May 19, 2014; David E. Sanger and Nicole Perlroth, "Chinese Army Unit Is Seen as Tied to Hacking Against U.S. Companies," *The New York Times*, February 18, 2013.

141 US Trade Representative, *2020 Report to Congress on China's WTO Compliance* (Washington, DC: Office of the US Trade Representative, 2021); World Intellectual Property Organization, *WIPO IP Facts and Figures: China 2020* (Geneva: WIPO, 2020).

142 Eva Dou, House of Huawei: The Secret History of China's Most Powerful Company (Portfolio, 2025).

143 Cisco Systems, Inc. v. Huawei Technologies Co., Ltd., 2:03-cv-00027 (E.D. Tex. 2003).

144 *2023 Annual Report* (Huawei Investment & Holding Co., Ltd., 2024), 10.

145 Dou, House of Huawei.

146 Scott Kennedy, "The Chinese EV Dilemma: Subsidized Yet Striking," Center for Strategic and International Studies, last updated June 28, 2024, https://www.csis.org/blogs/trustee-china-hand/chinese-ev-dilemma-subsidized-yet-striking.

147 Blade Battery Technology White Paper (BYD Company Limited, 2020).

148 Byron Hurd, "BYD Profits Plummet as China's Price War Hits the Top Player," *The Drive*, August 29, 2025, https://www.thedrive.com/news/byd-profits-plummet-as-chinas-price-war-hits-the-top-player.

149 World Trade Organization, *Subsidies and Countervailing Measures Agreement and China Notifications* (Geneva: WTO, 2020); Organisa-

tion for Economic Co-operation and Development, *Industrial Subsidies and State Support in China* (Paris: OECD, 2019).

150 McGee, Patrick. *Apple in China: The Capture of the World's Greatest Company*. New York: Scribner, 2025.

151 Dominic Gates, "Boeing Delivers First 737 Jet from Completion Center in China," *The Seattle Times*, last updated December 14, 2018, https://www.seattletimes.com/business/boeing-aerospace/boeing-set-to-deliver-first-737-jet-from-completion-center-in-china/#content.

152 David Dollar, "The APEC Summit: Step Forward or Backward for the Trans-Pacific Partnership?," Brookings Institution, November 2014.

153 "World Manufacturing Production Statistics," United Nations Industrial Development Organization, 2023.

154 Nicola Jones, "China Tops CO_2 Emissions," *Nature*, June 20, 2007, https://www.nature.com/news/2007/070618/full/news070618-9.html.

155 "CO2 Emissions by Country," Global Carbon Atlas, 2023, http://www.globalcarbonatlas.org/en/CO2-emissions.

156 Joshua M. Ferreri et al., "The January 2013 Beijing 'Airpocalypse' and Its Acute Effects on Emergency and Outpatient Visits at a Beijing Hospital," *Air Quality, Atmosphere & Health* 11, no. 3 (2017): 301–09, https://doi.org/10.1007/s11869-017-0538-0.

157 Jos Lelieveld et al., "The Contribution of Outdoor Air Pollution Sources to Premature Mortality on a Global Scale," *Nature* 525 (2015): 367–71, https://doi.org/10.1038/nature15371.

158 For examples of river-basin pollution documented during this period, see: Ministry of Environmental Protection of China, *China Environment Bulletin 2011* (Beijing: MEP, 2012); Elizabeth Economy, *The River Runs Black: The Environmental Challenge to China's Future*, 2nd ed.

(Ithaca: Cornell University Press, 2010); and Jonathan Watts, "China's Rivers: An Environmental Crisis," *The Guardian*, February 22, 2011.

159 Michael Greenstone, "Four Years After Declaring War on Pollution, China Is Winning," The University of Chicago EPIC Energy Policy Institute, March 12, 2018, https://epic.uchicago.edu/research/four-years-after-declaring-war-on-pollution-china-is-winning/.

160 *Under the Dome*, documentary film, directed by Chai Jing, released February 28, 2015.

161 *Solar PV Global Supply Chains* (International Energy Agency, 2022), https://www.iea.org/reports/solar-pv-global-supply-chains.

162 *Energy Technology Perspectives 2023* (International Energy Agency, 2023), https://www.iea.org/reports/energy-technology-perspectives-2023.

163 *WWEA Annual Report 2023: Record Year for Windpower* (World Wind Energy Association, 2024), https://www.wwindea.org/AnnualReport2023.

164 *Global EV Outlook 2025: Electric Vehicle Batteries* (International Energy Agency, 2025), https://www.iea.org/reports/global-ev-outlook-2025/electric-vehicle-batteries.

165 Reuters. "China's BYD Surges to 3.02 Million EV Sales in 2023, Surpassing Tesla's 1.81 Million." *Reuters*. January 2, 2024. https://www.reuters.com/markets/asia/chinas-byd-set-surpass-tesla-ev-sales-2023-01-02/.

166 Marta Pacheco, "China Dominating Soaring Global Clean-Tech Industry," *Euronews*, May 6, 2024, https://www.euronews.com/green/2024/05/06/china-dominating-soaring-global-clean-tech-industry.

167 Isabel Hilton, "How China Became the World's Leader on Renewable Energy," Yale School of the Environment, March 13, 2024, https://e360.yale.edu/features/china-renewable-energy.

168 "EU Launches Two Probes into China Solar Manufacturers," *Financial Times*, April 3, 2024, https://www.ft.com/content/5e677032-82c6-4761-9053-a441ef1a71c4.

169 Robert Lighthizer, "The Era of Offshoring U.S. Jobs Is Over," *The New York Times*, May 11, 2020, https://www.nytimes.com/2020/05/11/opinion/coronavirus-jobs-offshoring.html.

170 Andy Brailo et al., "Premier Data: The State of PPE Supply One Year into COVID-19," *Premier Inc.*, April 1, 2021, https://premierinc.com/newsroom/blog/premier-data-the-state-of-ppe-supply-one-year-in-to-covid-19.

171 "COVID-19: Opportunities to Improve Federal Response and Recovery Efforts," US Government Accountability Office, June 25, 2020, https://www.gao.gov/products/gao-20-625.

172 "REPowerEU: Joint European Action for More Affordable, Secure and Sustainable Energy," European Commission, press release, March 8, 2022, https://ec.europa.eu/commission/presscorner/detail/en/ip_22_1511.

173 Stephen Morgan et al., "The Economic Impacts of Retaliatory Tariffs on US Agriculture," US Department of Agriculture Economic Research Service, November 1, 2022, https://ers.usda.gov/publications/pub-details/?pubid=102979.

174 Congressional Research Service. *Farm Policy: USDA's 2018–2019 Trade Aid Package.* Washington, DC: CRS, January 17, 2020. https://crsreports.congress.gov/product/pdf/R/R45929.

175 Morgan et al., "The Economic Impacts of Retaliatory Tariffs."

176 Roland Rajah and Ahmed Albayrak, "China Versus America on Global Trade," Lowy Institute, January 2025, https://interactives.lowyinstitute.org/features/china-versus-america-on-global-trade/.

177 "F-35 Lightning II: Global Partnership," Lockheed Martin, company factsheet, 2023, https://www.lockheedmartin.com/en-us/products/f-35/f-35-global-partnership.html.

178 David H. Autor et al., "The China Shock: Learning from Labor-Market Adjustment to Large Changes in Trade," *Annual Review of Economics* 8 (2016): 205–40.

179 Michael J. Hicks and Srikant Devaraj, *The Myth and the Reality of Manufacturing in America* (Ball State University, Center for Business and Economic Research, 2015), https://conexus.cberdata.org/files/MfgReality.pdf.

180 Xiangming Chen and Youqin Huang, "China's Urbanization and Migration: Policy, Population, and Social Consequences," *Cities* 104 (2020): 102770, https://www.sciencedirect.com/science/article/abs/pii/S0166046220303239.

181 John Giles, Albert Park, and Fang Cai, "How Has Economic Restructuring Affected China's Urban Workers?" China Quarterly 185 (March 2006): 61–95.

182 Peter Navarro, *Death by China: Confronting the Dragon* (Prentice Hall, 2011).

183 Bernie Sanders, statement on trade policy, Congressional Record, vol. 161, no. 80 (May 22, 2015): S3321. (Full text available in Congressional Record, Government Printing Office archives.)

184 *Poverty and Shared Prosperity 2020: Reversals of Fortune* (World Bank Group, 2020), https://www.worldbank.org/en/publication/poverty-and-shared-prosperity.

185 "The World Bank in China: Overview," World Bank Group, last updated October 23, 2024, https://www.worldbank.org/en/country/china/overview.

186 "The World Bank in Viet Nam: Overview," World Bank Group, last updated May 9, 2025, https://www.worldbank.org/en/country/vietnam/overview.

187 *World Development Report 2020: Trading for Development in the Age of Global Value Chains* (World Bank Group, 2019), https://www.worldbank.org/en/publication/wdr2020.

188 Mary Amiti and Donald R. Davis, *Trade, Firms, and Wages: Theory and Evidence* (Federal Reserve Bank of New York and Columbia University, 2011), https://www.newyorkfed.org/medialibrary/media/research/economists/amiti/wages_amiti_davis.pdf.

189 Steve Johnson, "S&P 500 Trackers Hit a Record 27% of 2023 Equity ETF Flows," *Financial Times*, April 2, 2024, https://www.ft.com/content/4a9b70d7-f956-4ac7-b730-7ee3cafbd9e1.

190 Amiti and Davis, *Trade, Firms, and Wages.*

191 "S&P 500 Q4 2018 Buybacks Set 4th Consecutive Quarterly Record at $223 Billion; 2018 Sets Record $806 Billion," *PR Newswire*, March 25, 2019, https://www.prnewswire.com/news-releases/sp-500-q4-2018-buybacks-set-4th-consecutive-quarterly-record-at-223-billion-2018-sets-record-806-billion-300817734.html.

192 Joseph Dybisz, *Modernizing Trade Adjustment Assistance*, white paper (Northeast-Midwest Institute, 2019), https://www.nemw.org/wp-content/uploads/2019/09/Trade-Adjustment-Assistance-White-Paper.pdf.

193 Matthew Gardner, *Fortune 500 Companies Hold a Record $2.6 Trillion Offshore* (Institute on Taxation and Economic Policy, 2017), https://itep.org/wp-content/uploads/pre0327.pdf.

194 US International Trade Commission, "Cast Iron Pipe Fittings from China," Investigation Nos. 731-TA-278 and 731-TA-1064 (2003,

with 2024 updates), https://www.usitc.gov/publications/701_731/pub5576.pdf.

195 Alexander Hamilton, *Report on the Subject of Manufactures*, communicated to the House of Representatives, December 5, 1791.

196 Aaron Flaaen et al., "The Production Relocation and Price Effects of US Trade Policy: The Case of Washing Machines," *American Economic Review* 110, no. 7 (2020): 2103–127, https://www.aeaweb.org/articles?id=10.1257/aer.20190611.

197 Flaaen et al., "Production Relocation."

198 Gary Clyde Hufbauer and Euijin Jung, *Steel Profits Gain, but Steel Users Pay, Under Trump's Protectionism* (Peterson Institute for International Economics, December 2019).

199 Hufbauer and Jung, *Steel Profits Gain.*

200 Gary Clyde Hufbauer and Sean Lowry, *US Tire Tariffs: Saving Few Jobs at High Cost* (Peterson Institute for International Economics, 2012).

201 Gabrielle Coppola, "Once a Trump Favorite, Harley Now Feels the Pinch of the Trade War," *Bloomberg*, June 25, 2018, https://www.bloomberg.com/news/articles/2018-06-25/harley-davidson-to-shift-motorbike-production-to-counter-tariffs.

202 Coppola, "Once a Trump Favorite."

203 Robbie Minton and Mariano Somale, "Detecting Tariff Effects on Consumer Prices in Real Time," Board of Governors of the Federal Reserve System, May 9, 2025, https://www.federalreserve.gov/econres/notes/feds-notes/detecting-tariff-effects-on-consumer-prices-in-real-time-20250509.html.

204 Omar Barbiero and Hillary Stein, "The Impact of Tariffs on Inflation," Current Policy Perspectives, *Federal Reserve Bank of*

Boston, February 6, 2025, https://www.bostonfed.org/publications/current-policy-perspectives/2025/the-impact-of-tariffs-on-inflation.

205 Flaaen et al., "Production Relocation."

206 Hufbauer and Jung, *Steel Profits Gain.*

207 Hufbauer and Jung, *Steel Profits Gain.*

208 *Labor Force Characteristics by Race and Ethnicity, 2023*, Report 1109 (US Bureau of Labor Statistics, 2024), https://www.bls.gov/opub/reports/race-and-ethnicity/2023/#:~:text=groups%20in%20 2023.-,Composition%20of%20the%20labor%20force,(See%20 table%201.).

209 Bown, "US-China Trade War Tariffs."

210 Bown, "US-China Trade War Tariffs."

211 Arendse Huld and Qian Zhou, "China Manufacturing Industry Tracker," *China Briefing*, October 30, 2025, https://www.china-briefing.com/news/china-manufacturing-industry-tracker-2024-25/.

212 National Bureau of Statistics of China, Industrial Production Data, 2024-2025.

213 Huld and Zhou, "China Manufacturing Industry Tracker."

214 Gerard DiPippo et al., "Beyond Tariffs: What the US Can Learn from China's Industrial Playbook," RAND Corporation, April 17, 2025, https://www.rand.org/pubs/commentary/2025/04/beyond-tariffs-what-the-us-can-learn-from-chinas-industrial.html.

215 European Council, "25th EU-China Summit: EU Press Release," press release, July 24, 2025, https://www.consilium.europa.eu/en/press/press-releases/2025/07/24/25th-eu-china-summit-eu-press-release/.

216 Agatha Kratz et al., "Why Isn't Europe Diversifying from China?" Rhodium Group, December 2, 2024, https://rhg.com/research/why-isnt-europe-diversifying-from-china.

217 François Chimits, "Growing Asymmetry: Mapping the Import Dependencies in EU and US Trade with China," Mercator Institute for China Studies, October 1, 2024, https://merics.org/en/report/growing-asymmetry-mapping-import-dependencies-eu-and-us-trade-china.

218 Kratz et al., "Why Isn't Europe Diversifying."

219 Barbiero and Stein, "The Impact of Tariffs on Inflation."

220 Erica York and Alex Durante, "Trump Tariffs: Tracking the Economic Impact of the Trump Trade War," *Tax Foundation*, last updated November 17, 2025, https://taxfoundation.org/research/all/federal/trump-tariffs-trade-war.

221 Minton and Somale, "Detecting Tariff Effects on Consumer Prices."

222 "Where We Stand: The Fiscal, Economic, and Distributional Effects of All US Tariffs," The Budget Lab at Yale, April 2, 2025, https://budgetlab.yale.edu/research/where-we-stand-fiscal-economic-and-distributional-effects-all-us-tariffs-enacted-2025-through-april.

223 "US Tariffs: What's the Impact?" J.P. Morgan Global Research, October 30, 2025, https://www.jpmorgan.com/insights/global-research/current-events/us-tariffs.

224 Minton and Somale, "Detecting Tariff Effects on Consumer Prices."

225 The Budget Lab at Yale, "Where We Stand."

226 The Budget Lab at Yale, "Where We Stand."

227 Budgetary and Economic Effects of Increases in Tariffs Implemented Between January 6 and May 13, 2025 (Congressional Budget Office, 2025), https://www.cbo.gov/publication/61389.

228 Niall Ferguson, Empire: The Rise and Demise of the British World Order (Basic Books, 2003), 242–67.

229 James Fallows, "Containing Japan," *The Atlantic*, May 1989, https://www.theatlantic.com/magazine/archive/1989/05/containing-japan/376337.

230 Autor et al., "The China Shock," 205–40.

231 *Renewable Power Generation Costs in 2020* (International Renewable Energy Agency, 2021), 13, https://www.irena.org/publications/2021/Jun/Renewable-Power-Costs-in-2020.

232 United States Census Bureau, "U.S. International Trade in Goods and Services: Annual Revision," news release, *US Bureau of Economic Analysis*, news release, 2023, https://www.bea.gov/sites/default/files/2024-06/trad1324.pdf.

233 Shawn Donnan and Enda Curran, "The Global Economy Enters an Era of Upheaval," *Bloomberg*, September 18, 2023, https://www.bloomberg.com/graphics/2023-geopolitical-investments-economic-shift.

234 Franklin Eric Keller, "The United States and Industrial Policy: A Look Inside the CHIPS Program Office" (master's thesis, Harvard University, Division of Continuing Education, 2025), https://dash.harvard.edu/server/api/core/bitstreams/5de6b5d8-e147-415b-ac15-6daef7e035f8/content.

235 "Global Update: Paris Agreement Turning Point," Climate Action Tracker, December 2021, https://climateactiontracker.org/publications/the-climate-crisis-worsens-the-warming-outlook-stagnates/.

236 John Kerry, "Climate Diplomacy and the US-China Relationship," *Foreign Affairs*, September 2022.

237 International Renewable Energy Agency, *Renewable Power Generation Costs in 2020.*

238 Vedant Subramanian, "International Trade Tariffs Past and Present: A Review of Historical and 2025 US Tariff Impacts on Inflation, Consumption, Reshoring, and Substitution," *SSRN*, July 5, 2025, https://papers.ssrn.com/sol3/papers.cfm?abstract_id=5438034.

239 Laura Silver et al., "Negative Views of China Tie Near Historic Highs in Many Countries," Pew Research Center, June 29, 2023.

240 "American Public Opinion and US Foreign Policy 2023," Chicago Council on Global Affairs, September 2023. (2023 Chicago Council Survey.)

241 US Department of Agriculture, Agricultural Trade Data (China), 2023.

242 US Bureau of Economic Analysis, Direct Investment by Country Data, 2023.

243 Boeing, Market Outlook Data (China), 2023.

244 Ray Huang, 1587, A Year of No Significance: The Ming Dynasty in Decline (Yale University Press, 1981), 3.

245 Duncan Clark, *Alibaba: The House That Jack Ma Built* (Ecco, 2016), 89.

246 Lardy, *The State Strikes Back*, 35.

247 Lan, *How China Works*, 156–78.

248 Four Decades of Poverty Reduction in China: Drivers, Insights for the World, and the Way Ahead (World Bank Group, 2022).

249 Lardy, *The State Strikes Back*, 88.

250 *Open Doors 2023 Report on International Educational Exchange* (Institute of International Education, 2023).

251 "2020 Yearbook of Immigration Statistics," US Department of Homeland Security Office of Homeland Security Statistics, 2020, https://ohss.dhs.gov/topics/immigration/yearbook/2020.

www.ingramcontent.com/pod-product-compliance
Lightning Source LLC
LaVergne TN
LVHW091819070826
844874LV00004B/10

* 9 7 9 8 8 9 1 8 8 3 1 0 9 *